W9-BLJ-257

LAMBS ON THE LEDGE

*Seeing and Avoiding
Danger in Ministry*

Joyce Strong

Christian Publications
Camp Hill, Pennsylvania

Christian Publications
3825 Hartzdale Drive, Camp Hill, PA 17011

Faithful, biblical publishing since 1883

ISBN: 0-87509-650-6

© 1995 by Christian Publications
All rights reserved
Printed in the United States of America

95 96 97 98 99 5 4 3 2 1

Unless otherwise indicated,
Scripture taken from the HOLY BIBLE,
NEW INTERNATIONAL VERSION ®,
© 1973, 1978, 1984 by the
International Bible Society,
Used by permission of
Zondervan Publishing House.
All rights reserved.

DEDICATION

To the brave Lambs in ministry
who have learned to walk
in humility and obedience
even upon
the ledge

IN APPRECIATION

To my husband Jim
who has faithfully endured
my growing pains
and become my best friend;

To my children
Scott and Julie,
who have always believed in me;

To Brenda Hagadorn
who lovingly shared her computer
skills with me;

And

To my buddy Joy Weaver
who laughed and cried with me
every inch of the way.

The illustrations in this book are taken
from real life. They are composites
of many who, like me, have been or are
lambs on the ledge.

CONTENTS

FOREWORD

There is no higher calling in the will of God than to Christian ministry. But there is a price to be paid. Those who respond to the Savior's call to serve Him and His church will face difficulties, disappointments, temptations and sacrifices beyond human ability to cope. But with those pressures comes His gracious promise, "My grace is sufficient for you, for my strength is made perfect in weakness."

Like Moses, who continued to wear his veil after the glory had faded away, many of us in ministry have camouflaged weaknesses and tried to cover up our failures. Joyce Strong, having walked this difficult path herself, has blown our cover. With courage and compassion she deals with issues that, if left unreconciled, produce a myriad of problems.

Every Christian worker, at some point in their ministry, find themselves dangerously "on the ledge." The author's loving spirit, broad experience and grasp of biblical principles along with her gifted writing style, qualify her to point out how we may escape these dangers, rescue others from the ledge and help restore our wounded brothers and sisters.

This book contains truth that is desperately needed as we approach the end of the twentieth century. Anyone determined to be a man or woman of integrity will richly benefit from reading it. Those who are part of a ministry team or multi-staff church will find invaluable help. It should be required reading for ordinands and those preparing for full-time ministry.

We cannot deny that there are many "lambs on the ledge" but how reassuring to know that the Great Shepherd of the sheep is able to keep them from falling and to present them faultless before His presence.

Gordon M. Cathey

Minister for 46 years with
The Christian and Missionary Alliance

BEFORE DAWN

The silky blue-blackness of the night sky slowly gave way to gray, then yellow, tinged with pink. The dew danced on the green grass as the early morning sunlight slipped gently over the field.

The quiet pasture, jutting out from the rugged mountainside, contentedly rested above the deep, gloomy ravine that ran along its northern exposure.

The Shepherd had slept lightly. Between the threat of wolves and thieves and the flock's own strange compulsion to wander off—as if drawn by the music of some invisible Pied Piper—He was always ready for action.

As He mused over His charges, His eye caught an unnatural movement in the tough, dry mesquite bushes that thrived on the precipice of the ravine. The bushes were worthless to eat—although His lambs seemed never to be convinced of it until their mouths were sore and bleeding from chewing on them—and served only to hide predators.

The Shepherd moved quickly and cautiously beyond the drowsy sheep that lay near Him, toward the rustling bushes. Which would it be this time? A wolf? A snake? A thieving herdsman looking for a quick addition to his own flock?

Suddenly a rock and a large clump of earth, loosened by the commotion, tumbled from beyond the bushes and over the precipice. He could hear them thumping and scraping their way down the side of the ravine. With a dull thud, they hit the bottom.

Crouching down, the Shepherd parted the brittle thicket, one arm's length at a time. As He pressed through the dense growth dangerously close to the ragged edge of the ravine, His hands touched wool—the soft wool of one of His very own lambs!

Its back legs were over the edge, and sheer terror filled its wide eyes. In another moment, the loose earth under its upper body would break away and carry it down, down to its own demise.

The Shepherd stretched His body carefully over the weak earth, grasped the forelegs of the terrified lamb and slowly pulled its body fully onto solid ground. Within minutes, the lamb was in His arms, its heart pounding and its body shaking from fright. He held the lamb close until it calmed down.

As the Shepherd ran His hands over every part of the lamb's body, He found its leg was broken. He gently set the twisted leg, and then cradled the tired, dusty heap of wool in His strong arms.

"You will learn through the pain," whispered the Shepherd, as much to Himself as to the lamb, "to

*stay close to me." A sad smile played upon His face.
"You will learn."*

* * *

There are no innocents in the kingdom of
God—we are all wandering lambs. From Sunday
school teacher to pastor, elder to evangelist,
counselor to custodian and musician to deacon,
we all too often venture into the dry mesquite
bushes of disobedience—even if only in issues of
the heart. But that is, after all, where sin begins.

Christians in ministry are accused from time
to time of having it easy—that we are insulated
from the world, the flesh and the devil. But in
pursuing God's voice and His call to reach the
lost and encourage believers, we find ourselves
not in a fortress, but pastured, however lovingly, on a precarious plateau like ledge on the
mountainside. Temptation and deception stalk
us there perhaps more relentlessly than anywhere else. And if any one of us falls from that
ledge, hundreds—perhaps thousands—of others
may hear the cry of our demise and be shaken in
their faith.

It is an exposed position, facing in one direc-
tion the warmth of the sun and in the other the
frost of the canyon. While the camaraderie of fellow believers and the precious presence of God
lift us up through all the pressures and responsibilities of ministry, our flesh repeatedly threatens
to drag us down.

And in the shadows, studying us for any sign of rebellion, lurks the Pied Piper, Satan himself, the archenemy of our souls. He hates us with a passion, because we bear the image of God. That God delights in us galls him; he is committed to our spiritual destruction. To see us cast from the ledge of ministry through hatred and bitterness, weakness and disillusionment would bring him sadistic joy!

The Pied Piper plays a song that is sweet to our flesh. The discordant tones of self-righteous anger, jealousy, self-pity, ungratefulness and unforgiveness captivate our hearts all too easily. You would think that we in the ministry would be a tough lot to entice, but that is just not so.

However slippery the precipice or enticing the Piper's song, we fall into sin not because the Piper plays, but because we follow. We Christians are often frighteningly ignorant regarding the schemes and intrigues of our own hearts, until it is too late. We also underestimate the devil's hatred of us and our ease in believing lies. We think we are invincible!

Were it not for the Good Shepherd, Jesus Christ, who soundly stripped Satan of his power at Calvary, we would be no match for our ancient adversary and the machinations of our old nature. The cross destroyed the law that insisted that we would sin without reprieve. We *can* walk in obedience—even on the ledge of ministry!

Always, the love of God pursues us. Imagine: The eternal God—Creator of all there is, the final

Word on all mankind's schemes and the holy Judge of the earth—loves us! God will move heaven and earth to make the message of love and redemption clear. In every event of our lives, this message sings.

When we sin, conviction roars in our bones, and sweet forgiveness meets us upon our knees. The power of our sin to bind us is swept away in the joy of embracing Him again. And when we lift our eyes to heaven, His vast blueprint for our lives stretches across the sky. We rise with fresh vision and hope.

On the other hand, when we see the character flaws in the lives of those around us in ministry, we are amazingly quick to forget our own weaknesses—and God's generosity in forgiving us—and we play the critic. We shake our heads and wonder how on earth these people were ever allowed into Christian service in the first place! Many times we may ask ourselves, "Why didn't I ask more questions before joining up with this crew?"

When we suspect that principles are being violated, we hesitate confronting for fear of being judged unspiritual or being dismissed from the work we love so much, in the event we are wrong. Then, if we allow anger and bitterness to take root in our hearts, we won't dare speak up lest we expose our own nasty attitudes and be asked to repent instead!

Worse still, our vision may grow narrow in the night. Like the psalmist, we are tempted to say,

"Surely in vain have I kept my heart pure; in vain have I washed my hands in innocence" (73:13).

We are prone to take sides when there are conflicts within the ministry. It seems so important to determine who is right and who is wrong, who is anointed and who isn't, who should be doing what and who shouldn't. However, we are all in a common fix.

The fix is our desperate need for maturity. Too often we remain green, tense and self-absorbed, disregarding the provision within adversity that will make us grow up. Our flesh remains unbroken; the cross, a mere fixture on the wall.

At times we think that we alone know how things should be done. We become stubborn and unteachable. But only God has the Truth, and we *can* learn it. We need to rediscover *His* ways and abandon ours. Through yielding to a vision beyond our own, we see the point of it all—our maturity and the worship of God alone. When we learn this, our effectiveness in the ministry takes on a much deeper significance.

As we become convinced of His love for us in every situation, we can be brave enough to evaluate ourselves more accurately. Correction will begin to do its work in us, and we may even have a redemptive word for someone else who is dangerously close to a fall.

If we do not learn the lessons before us, life within the demands of ministry will forever be an epic of suffering and disillusionment. But our grief will be due only to our penchant for resisting the preparation, for facing life as though earth were all that mattered, and our own lordship all there were to revere!

We will fitfully pace the ledge, moving closer and closer to the precipice. And then we will hear it: the wind whispering through the eerie shadows of the chasm only inches away.

Lambs, beware!

DANGERS UPON THE LEDGE

Am I now trying to win the approval of men, or of God? Or am I trying to please men? If I were still trying to please men, I would not be a servant of Christ. (Galatians 1:10)

Fear of man will prove to be a snare,
  *but whoever trusts in the L*ORD *is kept safe*
        (Proverbs 29:25)

There is no fear in love. But perfect love drives out fear, because fear has to do with punishment. The one who fears is not made perfect in love.
  We love because he first loved us.
        (1 John 4:18-19)

Chapter 1

ᑭERFORMANCE ORIENTATION

The little sheep tried so hard to be a favorite. His legs ached from all the times he had jumped back and forth across the meadow stream to have strong legs like his father.

Every day he looked anxiously into his father's face for approval. Would he ever be sure he was really loved?

ᑭore and more men and women are coming into the church from backgrounds of abuse and rejection, never having felt that they were able to measure up in the eyes of those from whom they sought love as children. No matter what they did, they were put down. They perceive the Church as a haven, a place where they can perhaps finally win approval and feel good about themselves.

They are eager to please.

If they don't soon come to a revelation of God's complete acceptance of them simply because of Calvary, and that all He wants is their love, trouble is ahead. They will be attracted to others who are "great achievers" and try to imitate and please them. It seems like a good plan for being accepted. But before long, they will feel as empty as before. Their old patterns of performing for approval have only become religious.

The roots of religious performance orientation go down into the lie that the love of God and righteousness are something that can and must be earned. It insists that approval is everything and includes an inexhaustible list of good deeds.

It is legalism and works, with a new look.

I see you look away, and I hear you say
  You just can't try hard enough
  You just can't run far enough
For you hang your head in shame
  And stay buried in the pain
  Never being quite sure
  Never feeling secure . . .[1]

The little boy choked back fear as his dad pushed him out onto the platform.

"Come on, Jeffrey, the folks want to hear you sing! Do it for Jesus and for me," the energetic young pastor whispered into his son's ear. "Show 'em how good you are! We'll go out for ice cream after the service. OK?"

"Give the little guy a big hand, folks!" Applause erupted all over the auditorium as people eagerly leaned forward to be able to see the pastor's six-year-old son as he climbed onto a chair behind the microphone.

Jeffrey tried to see only ice cream cones, instead of all those faces out there. Somehow he found his voice as the piano began to play the song his dad had taught him. His dad's face beamed with obvious pride. And the people loved it.

When the service finally ended that night, only Jeffrey remembered the ice cream. His dad was busy making plans for the next service . . . and the next song Jeffrey could sing.

Twenty years later, Jeffrey has a ministry and great dreams of his own. He is a driven man; rarely does he rest. Even family vacations somehow turn into speaking engagements wherever they go.

His wife Elizabeth had always wanted to be a preacher's wife, and she is trying hard to keep up with all Jeffrey and the church expect of her. But Elizabeth is losing ground.

In spite of increasing headaches, she presses on—directing the choir, teaching Sunday school, speaking to women's groups, volunteering at the mission downtown and taking phone calls from hurting people—while her housework slides and private time with God slips away.

One gray morning, while Jeffrey is in another state speaking at a missions conference, the ambulance pulls up to the parsonage. Elizabeth's best friend Kate has called for help.

Elizabeth can't remember her name.

> *You are not so weak*
> *I cannot make you strong*
> *You are not so weary*
> *I cannot help you to go on . . .*
> *O My precious lamb*
> *Turn your eyes above*
> *It's just because of who you are*
> *You have inherited My love . . .*[2]

Many of us in ministry unwittingly model performance orientation to our families, as well as to new Christians in the church. Instead of trying to please and gain approval from demanding parents, we work to please and gain approval from God and the Body of Christ. The whole idea is that if we can perform well enough to please those whom we serve or admire, we are of value. We will work very hard, especially publicly.

What we *do* is noble: soul winning, building big ministries to help people, giving every moment of our waking hours to the concerns of "the ministry" (often to the neglect of our own devotions, health and families); but our *motivation* (to gain approval and righteousness) is warped.

If gaining approval requires a false front, we will wear it, because approval is everything. However, after a while we lose track of who we are! But the mask can't be let down. All would be lost if people knew how empty we felt inside. Fear of rejection and escalating pride (in all we "do" for the Kingdom) hold the mask in place. Meanwhile, we begin to resent the taskmaster we mistakenly perceive God to be.

> *In your struggle for perfection*
> *Many times you fall*
> *But do you know my love*
> *would be the same*
> *If you never changed at all . . .*[3]

Unfortunately, we gain the applause of men while knowing we are not what we seem. Everyone knows that hypocrisy stinks, but to be praised while stinking really confuses one's spirit.

Down deep, where the Holy Spirit has taken up residence by virtue of salvation, sooner or later there comes a scream for the train to stop so we can get off. However, the stronger the religious spirit and the need to maintain admiration through outstanding performance, the more difficult it is to stop. It feeds upon itself, and others encourage its growth through praise.

The power and control gained through our accomplishments are nearly impossible to relinquish! How could we face life without others' approval and admiration? Who would we be?

The irony is that we can never quite make it to perfection and we are never truly secure. No amount of religious fervor delivers us from the old problems of anger, fear of rejection, a critical spirit, unforgiveness, feelings of worthlessness and confusion. Thus, we fail, and we feel that we are constantly disappointing God. Our answer: Try harder. Do more. Perform better next time.

And it hurts me when I see you
  Let your fear and pride keep you away
Don't measure My favor by what
  you have done
But by the promises that I have
  made . . .[4]

In this issue of performance, Christian teen-agers are often unwittingly more perceptive than we adults. Most rebellion by teens in the church is simply their way of saying, "I refuse to play the game. Love me for who I am, not for all the perfect things you can get me to do. I won't believe that God loves me uncondition-ally until *you* do!"

Many of us must repent of believing the lies that we can earn God's approval, that our worth depends upon what we do and the praise we re-ceive. We must also forgive parents and other authority figures who planted the lie within us in the first place. If we don't, we will be candidates for two options: committing some shocking sin so that the charade can end or having an emo-tional or physical breakdown when the weight of performing becomes unbearable.

Though your mistakes often bind you
  Put them all behind you
Don't let them keep you from me
Let these arms hold you
  Let my love enfold you
Open your heart and receive . . .[5]

Lambs, God loves us! We can be at rest because the Shepherd paid for our acceptance in full at Calvary. He cares not about what amazing things we can do or who is impressed with us. He cares only that we long to know Him intimately, love Him with abandonment and listen for His voice.

He will give us peace and security, even on *the ledge*.

> *Come closer, closer to me*
> *Look in my eyes, and you will see*
> *My love is a love that just begins*
> *At the place where your understanding*
> *ends!*[6]

Endnotes

1. "Come Closer," ©1995 Leslie Ludy. From *His Gentle Ways* by Eric & Leslie Ludy. Used by permission.
2. Ibid.
3. Ibid.
4. Ibid.
5. Ibid.
6. Ibid.

*My brothers, as believers in our glorious Lord Je-
sus Christ, don't show favoritism. Suppose a man
comes into your meeting wearing a gold ring and
fine clothes, and a poor man in shabby clothes also
comes in. If you show special attention to the man
wearing fine clothes and say, "Here's a good seat for
you," but say to the poor man, "You stand there" or
"Sit on the floor by my feet," have you not discrimi-
nated among yourselves and become judges with
evil thoughts?* (James 2:1-4)

*The man of integrity walks securely,
    but he who takes crooked paths will
        be found out.* (Proverbs 10:9)

*Here is a trustworthy saying: If anyone set his
heart on being an overseer, he desires a noble task.
Now the overseer must be above reproach. . . . He*

must not be a recent convert (novice, KJV), or he may become conceited and fall under the same judgment as the devil. . . . They must first be tested; and then if there is nothing against them, let them serve . . . (1 Timothy 3:1-2, 6, 10)

Chapter 2

FAVORITISM AND PREMATURE ELEVATION

The young apprentice shepherd was a curious fellow. His skill on the harp was charming, and his confidence knew no bounds. But he seemed ignorant of the most ordinary things! He didn't know a wolf from a dog, he slept too soundly, frequently forgot to check the sheep's ears for ticks at the end of the day and limped from an unattended wound.

Marcy and John McKinney had been on the mission field for several years. They came home for a rest, fully expecting and desiring to return to the field as soon as possible. However, the pastor of the church they began attending thought that they would be the perfect ones to inaugurate a missions school in their church.

Because the pastor had been showing them a great deal of special attention, giving them access to his life that was denied others, they let his counsel overrule what they had previously planned to do. He persuaded them to stay at home to establish this training program, turning down the foreign mission opportunity for which they had been waiting.

They worked tirelessly to reach the pastor's goal, faithfully challenging people in the church to become interested in missions and involved in the training program. However, any progress was short-lived.

To their dismay, Marcy and John soon found it difficult to get in to see the pastor. He was busy.

They began to feel cast off because they couldn't produce what he wanted. Their own vision was past retrieving, and they eventually left the church altogether. The pastor couldn't even be reached so that they could say goodbye properly. They wondered if they would ever be able to trust the guidance of a pastor again.

Furthermore, because of the special attention given them while there, many of the church members resented Marcy and John. People whom they needed as friends during this time were distant. They were suddenly very much alone.

*   *   *

Favoritism in ministry is an insidious evil. It divides the ranks, engenders jealousy and envy, confuses discipline, and isolates and weakens the favorite as he takes his eyes off Jesus and becomes attached to a man. It inevitably causes others to feel judged and rejected by the leader who is showing the favoritism.

Mentoring Versus Favoritism

Mentoring and showing favoritism can easily be mistaken for each other, but they are two vastly different things.

Mentoring is when a young believer seeks the wisdom and discipling of a more mature believer. It is an agreement by mutual consent, for a specified period of time, with the desired result being his maturity and dependence upon God alone.

If it is entered into because the mentoree has a great hunger to grow spiritually, important correction is likely to be received, not resisted. The results can be gratifying as the mentoree welcomes from the mentor both instruction and discipline.

Favoritism, however, is selecting someone for special attention. It can occur in any ministry setting. Often favoritism is based upon co-dependency: the leader seeking to rescue or be needed, and the favorite seeking to be loved and accepted. Sometimes it is a way in which an insecure leader begins to surround himself with dependent, indebted people who won't oppose him. Or it can be a way to use talented people to fulfill a leader's own agenda.

Favoritism is particularly devastating in a smaller, close-knit ministry, such as a residential discipleship program. In such a close community, everyone knows what is going on and is likely to fixate upon it. It becomes a consuming concern.

For a long period of time, favoritism—in the name of mentoring—occurred in a residential ministry in which I served. Many of the rules were suspended for the favorite. He got to go places and do things that the other student residents couldn't, spending coveted time with the leader. This, of course, gave rise to jealousy and envy among the other residents, who wanted to spend time with him as well. The favorite soon found himself alienated from his peers, talked about and even hated. He missed out on valuable friendships and the power of the program in exchange for the special attention of the leader.

If the student could have successfully completed the program under the same conditions as everyone else and then sought discipling or mentoring, it would have worked well. As it was, the staff felt betrayed and undermined, since they were left to settle disputes and deal with bad attitudes among the other residents—all resulting from the inequity of the situation. Staff members were caught in the middle—frustrated, having to somehow defend what was tearing them all apart.

There was no improvement in the favored resident's attitude during this tense time; all the character weaknesses and bitterness that had made him a candidate for an intense discipleship program in the first place surfaced repeatedly. I believe the leader himself eventually recognized that favoring the resident did more harm than good, but by then it was too late to make him begin the program all over again. He had to be withdrawn from the program for everyone's sake.

What grieved me the most was that while the resident had come into the program because he needed the discipline and training that it offered, he was ultimately deprived of it. My concern for this young man was even greater than my concern for the frustrated staff and confused students.

There had never been a need for the leader to go around his staff to mentor a student who was still in the program. A better investment of time would have been to disciple staff members, who were themselves in need of grooming. The time the leader spent with the student had actually been stolen from that which had been due the staff.

As the ministry leader recognized the problem, the practice of trying to mentor students within the program was stopped, and God poured out His blessing on the ministry. The enemy's deception has been broken and the effectiveness of the ministry has been multiplied!

Equality and Respect

I am convinced that proper respect for those who minister and equal treatment of those who receive ministry bear good fruit. If a leader diligently nurtures and teaches his staff, always treating them with consideration even when correcting, the staff will be equipped to do the same for those served by the ministry. It really works! Staff need the director's confidence and respect even more than the students do. *A well-cared-for staff produces a well-cared-for ministry. As a result, confidence and respect then travel easily back up the chain of command to the leader.*

If a leader finds it necessary to intervene in a staff member's handling of a person or situation, the staff member should be included in the process and given opportunity to learn from it. A leader who undermines the people he or she leads is destroying the effectiveness of their ministry. Herein is a common wounding of staff that should not be.

A leader's mentoring should be limited to a novice staff member, an intern or someone else who is in a ministry position and has a legitimate reason to be with the mentor. As mentioned earlier, it will be much more effective if sought by the mentoree, rather than imposed by the mentor.

Principles for Mentoring

Whether mentoring is done by pastors, ministry leaders, staff members, lay leaders or any other mature Christians, cautions are in order and planning is important for everyone's safety. The lives of both the mentor and mentoree are precious and must be protected. The principles that follow apply not only to mentoring, but to any ongoing counseling situation.

No matter what the ministry setting, mentoring will work only if the mentoree has a sincere desire to grow strong in God. If he merely wants the attention of the mentor or seeks to derive his identity from the relationship, nothing but frustration will be produced, especially for the mentor.

Goals should be clearly defined, and a time frame for re-evaluation and completion established. The mentor must remember always that it is not his or her task to "save" the mentoree or become the mentoree's final authority on personal or spiritual matters. The mentor's job should always be to point the young believer to dependence upon God and His Word, leading the mentoree into deeper understanding through wisdom and experience.

The mentoree should be encouraged to become involved with other Christians and not be exclusively bound to the mentor. The mentoree must pursue the goal of standing on his or her own spiritual legs, not becoming dependent on the mentor for every decision.

If either the mentor or mentoree is married, the spouse should be consulted, considering the amount of time mentoring will necessitate. It is also wise for the mentoring pair to be accountable to a pastor or some other third party. This will protect them both from unhealthy motives or excessive closeness.

Furthermore, a mentor who is married must guard against sharing intimate facts about his or her life that should be shared only with a spouse or a counselor. Such confidences produce an emotional bonding with the mentoree that moves beyond the mentoring plan and endangers all other relationships, especially those with spouse and children. It also prevents the proper separation that should occur when the time agreed upon for the mentoring expires.

It is also not wise for the mentor to give material gifts to the mentoree; such action makes others (including the mentor's family) jealous and short-circuits dependence upon God's provision through prayer.

Even the best pastors and lay leaders may have unhealthy patterns of control in their lives. Our influence may prove toxic to the very people we are trying to help. Instead of setting them free to think and respond to God for themselves, we may cause them to be indebted and bound to us. The bottom line? If our hidden reason for mentoring is to be needed, to be someone's savior, we need counseling ourselves and we should not be afraid to seek it.

Premature Elevation

The platform lights in the sanctuary dimmed as Barclay closed out the service with an altar call. The piano played softly and scores of weeping men and women poured down the center aisle to make peace with God.

A wave of satisfaction swept over his six-foot, husky frame. He was a giant of a man. Barclay had proven once again that he had the "right stuff" to preach.

Saved dramatically from a life of drugs and alcohol, he had been a Christian for only two years when the elders of this church called him last September to lead their evangelism campaign. They had been so impressed with his powerful presence and dynamic preaching style that they had voted him in after hearing him only twice! He would do his best not to disappoint them.

Back in his office, he tossed his suit coat over the arm of one of the two leather chairs facing his desk, loosened his tie and closed the door. He strode across the room to his book closet.

The phone rang, startling him.

Janie's voice sounded lonely and plaintive on the other end. "Honey, it's late. The kids are already in bed. Hurry home, please?"

"Sure, Babe," he answered carefully, trying to keep the edge off his voice. "Just let me unwind here at the office for a few minutes. It's been a pressure-filled day, and I'm kinda hyped up.

"I'll be there in a little while. Go to sleep. I'll wake you when I get there," he said gently.

There was silence on the other end.

"Give me some space, okay?" Now he was irritated.

Click. She had hung up. They'd been through this before.

Barclay heaved a sigh, then turned back to the closet. He pulled a tape out from behind a stack of commentaries and inserted it into the VCR perched atop the small TV he had by his desk.

Kicking off his shoes, he settled into his chair and pushed the buttons.

The images from the lurid porno film surged through his senses. He hated this side of himself. He was hooked, and he knew it. It was an addiction that had begun when he was 15, when his street buddies had taken him into a peep show for the first time. He had been hiding it ever since.

His rise in the ministry had been so rapid, there had been no time to deal with the demon inside. Many times he had longed to get help, but the demands of the church left him with little energy to find a counselor with whom he felt comfortable.

Unknown to Barclay, his office door was being opened by an unexpected guest. An elder had been looking for him. While the tape rolled, the horrified elder stared in astonishment at the scene before him.

*   *   *

"He must not be a novice. . . ."

How often have we seen novices whose personal lives were questionable put into roles of influence over others! This is dangerous for everyone.

Tempting Danger

A pastor, for instance, must resist the temptation to elevate a talented or charismatic new Christian to a position of leadership. It is easy for the pastor to lose focus and have his eye on the pressing needs of his own programs rather than on what would be best for the young believer and the church in the long run. Those who are novices—or even those who have been saved for some time but are newcomers to the church—should first be given the opportunity to become part of the entire body and to learn to esteem others above themselves. God is not in a hurry. Often flaws are exposed during the waiting period—either in the pastor's plan or in the newcomer's character. It is at the heart of the Shepherd's plan to allow a novice time to get a good footing spiritually and to mature personally. God is more concerned with character than with programs and personalities.

From the other perspective, new Christians must resist the temptation to allow their dazzling testimony and natural charm to be "used" by a ministry. It would be wise for young believers to stay behind the scenes for at least a year, while being discipled and getting counseling for any root problems they might have.

A good preparation for ministry is to learn to work hard, sweat honestly for a living, pay bills, respect authority, raise a loving family and be a good neighbor. The more naturally talented a person is, the more easily he or she could fall prey to pride if cast into the limelight before learning these lessons. A humiliating fall would not be far away.

Many new believers—with dynamic testimonies, intellects or talents—have been set up for

disaster by either favoritism or premature eleva-
tion to public ministry. They were reborn in their
spirits but were still unbroken and undisciplined
in their flesh. Because they were, at first, so ad-
mired by others, they thought they had "arrived"
and could function as if they had been walking
with God for many years.

When they found they still had great inner
struggles and bad habit patterns, they were not
only disillusioned with God's work in them, but
unable to go to anyone for help because of their
pride. After all, they were leaders! At that point,
the fall was close at hand.

*   *   *

The board of elders met the next day. Barclay
was fired. No one was prepared to help him; they
were still in shock.

This would be the last straw for Janie. She had
taken all she could before he became a Christian.
He would be back on the street tomorrow.

As the stunned Barclay stumbled from the
room, the rest of the men stared awkwardly at the
floor.

*   *   *

"He must not be a novice. . . "

Sadly, when prematurely-elevated leaders fall
and their sins are exposed, those who had previously praised them usually desert them out of

embarrassment. Too often, especially if they had been saved from off the streets, they end up back there on drugs and alcohol, worse than they ever were before.

Those responsible for hiring personnel must be committed to them and their ongoing health in the ministry. Regular communication, counseling and prayer should be routine to *prevent* falls and to deal with any twists in the person's life that might surface later.

The health of those in ministry must be pursued with great diligence, both by the men and women themselves and by those who hire them. Their maturity will be of greater benefit to the Body than all the talent they can display.

Jesus said to them, "The kings of the Gentiles lord it over them; and those who exercise authority over them call themselves Benefactors. But you are not to be like that. Instead, the greatest among you should be like the youngest, and the one who rules like the one who serves. For who is greater, the one who is at the table or the one who serves? Is it not the one who is at the table? But I am among you as one who serves." (Luke 22:25-27)

Ill-gotten treasures are of no value,
*   but righteousness delivers from death.*
The LORD does not let the righteous go hungry,
*   but he thwarts the craving of the wicked.*
     (Proverbs 10:2–3)

Chapter 3

LEADERSHIP: POWER, POSITION AND MONEY

The golden-fleeced lamb was the largest in any hord that grazed upon the ledge. He was strong, and he sensed his power over the weaker, more slightly-built sheep around him.

He eyed the brush upon the northern rim. He was surely tough enough to eat what the others couldn't! He ambled away from the flock, unnoticed by the rest who contentedly grazed facing the southern mountains.

What causes some of us to become little kings when we reach the "throne" of leadership? Whatever causes us to consider thrones in the first place?

It is amazing how quickly, after having been assigned a leadership position, we forget that authority is given by God alone. We also forget that we don't, and never will, own our positions, and that God can remove us from them anytime He sees fit.

Why is it so difficult for us as leaders to admit it when we have been wrong, and then let the situation teach us again the nature of repentance? Transparency seems such a frightening prospect to us. It appears that we somehow think the rules are different for us.

*   *   *

Pastor Marvin Baker's church was in a mess. "There's got to be a way to fix it," he muttered as he reworked the figures on the pad before him on his office desk.

He had built this church from scratch and by last year, it was bursting at the seams. His dream of having the largest church in this part of the state was about to come true! He immediately sought plans and bids from contractors to double the size of the sanctuary and add on more classrooms and a gymnasium for the Christian school he'd always wanted.

The problems began, however, when one of the elders suggested that, instead of going into debt for a massive building program, they divide the congregation. The families who lived farthest west could be released to start another church in a town closer to them, some 25 miles from the present church. Half of the elders, he suggested, could also be released to oversee its formation. The associate pastor, Tom Craig, who had been on board for many years and was very competent, could pastor it. There was an auditorium available for them to rent until they were able to put the money together to buy or build.

The very thought of giving up half of his congregation right when he was on the brink of making quite a name for himself made the bile rise in his stomach. He wouldn't let it happen! This was his church, and it would stay his church!

So he fought the plan with every weapon of persuasion he had. And he won. The building began. The elders were disgruntled, but they knew Pastor Baker couldn't be stopped once his mind was made up.

Since then, petty disagreements had erupted throughout the church, and many families had pulled out. The rest were angry that they'd be stuck footing the bill for an enormous sanctuary they no longer needed.

*   *   *

I don't believe that God cares much about our levels of earthly position. I'm certain that He is grieved when they matter so much to His people.

Position does not translate into power in the kingdom of God. How wise He was to give His mighty power first to simple fishermen! He knows what a propensity we have for assuming ownership of power—if it merits prestige as well.

Jesus said that the first (in earth's economy) will be last (in heaven's economy), and the last, in the same manner, will be first. With that statement, He makes it logically impossible for us to concern ourselves with how we are positioned in a church or ministry—or anywhere else, for that matter. We are not due a favored position in even so much as the grocery line. What does it matter?

Will a "higher" position help us love God more? Will it make us more sensitive to the needs around us? Actually, the man who loves best is he who has repented and been forgiven most. There is no consideration of position. How all Christendom longs to see men in high positions teach us how to repent by example!

Nevertheless, in spite of all the inherent pitfalls, positions of leadership are necessary in earthly ministry. Jesus led His disciples. Cornelius led his legion. We all, in some way, lead someone. But *how* did Jesus, our only proper example, do the leading?

It seems that the "children" ranked highest in Jesus' eyes. He challenged the disciples to follow a child's example of transparency, tenderness and trust. He led them in exactly these qualities. Rank never turned Him arrogant; the crowd's applause never tempted Him to take a bow; He was never too busy to touch a leper. He knew always that the only thing worth teaching was what the Father revealed to Him to be true.

He remained in the position He had been in when He welcomed the children—on His knees as a servant. He expects no less from leaders today. In God's inverted pyramid of power, the leader is at the bottom with many dirty feet to lovingly wash.

We as leaders—whether as pastors, volunteer Sunday school teachers, elders or any other position of authority—are responsible to detect and warn against the Pied Piper and his song. Because of this, we have an enormous need to be ourselves undefiled within and to be held accountable to remain that way. We must come to understand that any sin left to fester in our own lives will pass its death out into everyone we serve!

When we allow arrogance into our hearts, the people under our authority will soon become arrogant. If we are hiding any kind of sin, it won't be long before those under us are doing the same thing. If we harbor bitterness against God or others, however cleverly masked by endless service, the people around us will soon find bitterness in their own hearts.

Repentance is Crucial

A dirty vessel cannot pour forth clean water. The only way to stop the flow of sin is repentance leading to change. Then, instead of defilement being multiplied into the Body of Christ, repentance and revival will sweep over everyone like a warm spring rain after a desolate winter.

As leaders, we must keep ourselves constantly accountable to someone who knows us thoroughly and isn't afraid to tell us the truth. The cry for God to search our hearts must always rise from our chambers. Cleanness before God and His people must matter more to us than all the "power" in the world.

When there is unforgiveness, unresolved family conflict, bitterness or an unwillingness to repent and obey God in any facet of our lives, it would be better to let our area of ministry close down than to have us remain defiled and continue to defile others. It is simply love for everyone that would prompt our release from responsibility until the problems are resolved God's way.

Until we understand God's idea of servanthood and His hatred of sin "in the camp," we may be doing more harm than good in the ministry. How we value others and honor our God with obedience in the inner man is of the utmost gravity.

And when we truly know *His* power, our hands will always be open, never grasping at ministry. To give it up, if necessary, would take nothing from us, for it was never ours to begin with! God's opinion is finally all that matters.

✳ ✳ ✳

The service was over. The guests—a team of young men who had ministered to the congregation—were chatting with folks in little groups all over the sanctuary. Voices gently rose and fell in prayer and in pleasant conversation.

Jack, the team leader, excused himself and slipped away to meet Pastor Mason in the church office behind the sanctuary. The pastor was beaming.

"Good job! The guys' testimonies were a great encouragement to us tonight. We'd love to have you back again real soon."

"Well, we sure love sharing with you folks. It's like home to us here," replied Jack warmly.

The pastor cleared his throat. "You know, the elders are seriously considering including your ministry in our missions budget! That's good news, isn't it?"

Jack smiled and grabbed the pastor's hand. "It sure is! Finances have been pretty lean lately. That would be such a blessing!"

"Well, thanks again. Here's the love offering from tonight. Have a safe trip back to the ministry."

Reverend Mason handed Jack the evening offering enclosed in an unmarked white envelope. Jack slipped it into his vest pocket and said his last goodbyes. Before leaving the building, he stepped into the men's room down the hall and closed the door. The thick envelope felt heavy in his pocket. "It wouldn't hurt to count it," he thought.

Th envelope contained $450 in checks and $98.50 in cash. Jack whistled softly. "Not bad for a little church on a Sunday night." He hadn't expected that much.

As he prepared to leave the men's room, he hesitated and then shifted two twenties into his back pocket. He had worked hard that day, driven 250 miles between services and missed precious time with his family.

"An extra good service merits a bonus, I'd say!" he whispered lightly to himself as he straightened his tie.

But suddenly, as his shoes touched the loose gravel of the parking lot, his heart started pounding.

"What on earth am I doing? God, I'm sorry, I'm sorry!" he cried softly as his eyes filled with tears. "Forgive me! Keep me from stealing from You!"

As fast as he could, he yanked the bills from his pants pocket and inserted them back into the white envelope.

* * *

Many parachurch ministries and small churches have never established a way to hold the person handling the offering accountable. The pastor, staff member or director has direct access to the money from the collection, and no one else is consistently present to count and record the amount received. In such cases, the temptation is always there to "skim off the top"—to steal.

Handling money can be dangerous. Money represents power, and—particularly for people with unresolved personal conflicts—power is furtively sought.

What would breed within a staff member the desire to steal?

- discontentment with salary
- envy of those in authority

- feelings of mistreatment or being taken advantage of by authority
- poor management of his own finances, which has caused him to live under stress

An early warning sign in some cases is when a staff member begins cutting corners on the time given to the ministry. If he comes in late, leaves early, stretches lunch breaks or errands, he is already a thief. A leader wisely said recently, "If a staff member begins stealing time, it won't be long before he steals money."

Likewise, what would breed thievery in a leader?

- assumption of "ownership" of the ministry
- belief that he is above any law that is applied to those under his authority
- resistance to correction by others regarding his "vision" or agenda; determination to make things happen
- neglect of counsel
- poor management of his personal finances, causing him to live under stress

※　※　※

Of course, the style of stealing may be different for the head of a ministry than for the staff. Instead of personally skimming or cheating, he may simply give funds that had been designated for one project to another project for which he has more concern. There may be seemingly good reasons for doing this; however, the fact remains that it was stolen from its original destination and people have been misled. The root of such behavior is arrogance. Such lawlessness will produce anarchy in time.

Judas, the treasurer of Jesus' ministry on earth, was an interesting, but tragic, figure. He had two obvious problems: He was a thief, but more importantly, he had an agenda of his own that he expected Jesus to follow.

He banked heavily on Jesus behaving according to his plan for amassing world power. He had figured that the small amount of cash he was skimming off would matter little after they took over. In his mind, they already possessed the wealth of the world, so the rules would be theirs to make. He was just a step ahead of them in the arena of power brokerage.

All Judas' energy went into preparation for prestige and earthly power. When Jesus refused the throne, Judas' heart was so filled with outrage, he was driven to avenge his losses. Hence, the betrayal scene.

Naturally he sold Jesus for whatever he could yet salvage of his financial empire. Revenge had to involve the root of it all—money and power.

He—a faceless unknown until then—brought down a King. And his reward necessarily had to be in the form of money; but the smallness of the amount was meant to scream out how worthless he believed a kingdom other than that of power and wealth to be.

He despised the kingdom of God. Therein was

his doom sealed.

The lesson: God is not our lackey. It is not His job to set us up with power and position. His kingdom's coinage is His Son's blood, which buys what money never could: the eternal salvation of a man's soul. He will move with holy power as He wills, without regard for men's plans. When we find money or power in our hands, we must daily disavow ownership of it—and nail our flesh fast to the cross.

It is important that each of us take a "reality check" regularly. If our attitude has become sour toward authority or the ministry, we'd better let the bitterness go, forgive and set things right. If we have stolen *anything*, we must repent, confess it to our authority or to the board and embrace whatever discipline is deemed appropriate. We must forget our pride!

All of us need accountability. Let's request it! Our lives are too precious to be prostituted to power and money. If we operate without accountability, our own lawlessless will cast us off the ledge.

An Important Note to Leaders

To promote the health of the ministry, leaders should meet regularly and individually with the staff who report to them. Such meetings give the opportunity to staff members to share safely anything that is bothering them and for the leader to help and encourage them in every way possible. An enormous number of misunderstandings and personal problems can be resolved, or even avoided, in such an open atmosphere. Caring communication and prayer for one another is the best preventive medicine for what ails most ministries today.

When you listen to a staff member, pray for and counsel him or her, you are saying that he or she is valued and loved. And as trust grows, such interrelating provides an opportunity for a leader to hold a staff member accountable for personal and spiritual growth.

The leader, in turn, needs someone—or better still, a small group of peers—committed to giving honest support and correction to one another. The members of such a group can pray daily for each other and meet at regular intervals to share problems and insight. In such a group, there is great practical help.

In especially difficult situations, a ministry should have a list of approved professional Christian counselors from which any staff member may draw. It is not a sign of weakness for anyone to take advantage of counseling. It is foolishness not to do so.

Making provision for your own well-being and that of your staff takes time, but the time must be carved out of even the busiest schedule. The "business" of a ministry is *never* more important than even one of its members.

Ministry is "people," and we cannot give any more health to those outside our organization than we possess ourselves.

*Another thing you do: You flood the LORD's altar
with tears. You weep and wail because he no longer
pays attention to your offerings or accepts them with
pleasure from your hands. You ask, "Why?" It is because the LORD is acting as the witness between you
and the wife of your youth, because you have broken
faith with her, though she is your partner, the wife of
your marriage covenant.*

*Has not the LORD made them one? In flesh and
spirit they are his. And why one? Because he was
seeking godly offspring.* **So guard yourself in your
spirit,** *and do not break faith with the wife of your
youth.* (Malachi 2:13-16, author's emphasis)

Chapter 4

DEADLY DECEPTION: SPIRITUAL ADULTERY

The sleek, gray snake slithered across the rocks at the water's edge. Two sheep, engrossed in studying their own and each other's reflections in the stream, didn't notice as he slid beneath their tender bellies and prepared to strike.

As her fingers eased over the piano keys, repeating gently the notes of the last chord of "Purify My Heart," Karen knew in her spirit that many had been touched by the worship this evening. A lingering smile sent her way from Wes, the worship team leader, confirmed it.

Karen slid quietly off the piano bench and headed for the music office. She glanced at her watch. If her husband Marty had been here, he would have been irritated that the music had taken so much time. He was always in a hurry to get home to his computer and *The Wall Street Journal*. She sighed.

"What was that sigh for?" asked Wes, who had been following her down the dimly lit hall of the Sunday school wing. "A pretty lady like you shouldn't have a care in the world! And your piano playing was . . . was . . . how can I describe the beauty and majesty you draw from those keys? Just being on the same team with you has been a thrill for me."

Karen slowed her steps to match his.

"So what was that sigh all about? You can tell me. We've been friends for too long to have secrets."

The soft tones of his voice, his physical closeness, the shadow of his strong, lean frame cast down the hall by the single light behind them brought a great longing for his touch.

Marty never thought of comforting or understanding her, she thought to herself wryly. He was in another world, a world of business deals and big bucks. He figured she was strong enough to take care of herself.

Well, she wasn't strong enough, and the load of loneliness had become too heavy. Surely God had sent Wes to let her know that her life was really of value to someone.

So she poured out her heart to him. And for the first time, Wes reached out and drew her into his arms as she cried.

Together, Karen and Wes stepped closer to the rim of *the ledge.*

*   *   *

It begins innocently enough. There's no plan to entice or injure anyone, just a desire to express how one feels.

"You are special, really special! I've never met anyone before who understands me like you do!"

Or simply, "What fun we have together!"

Something springs to life within us at these words and the connection is made. There's just one problem: One or both of us are married—to someone else.

The temptation to allow someone into our hearts who has no right to be there lurks in every role of ministry. Worship leaders, musicians, youth ministers, pastors, secretaries and counselors are yielding to it in alarming numbers. It most often occurs between a man and a woman, but it can also take root between two men, or two women. It is rarely discerned until it turns sexual.

Personal Testimony

I learned of spiritual adultery the hard way—by succumbing to it myself. Oddly, it overtook me at a time when I was very confident of my love for God and my devotion to my family.

True, my husband and I had endured some rocky times, with both of us wishing we had mar-

ried someone more sensitive to our needs. But at
this particular time, we had settled into the way
things were. Problems in our marriage were "under control," and we seemed quite happy. I was
trusting God that our relationship would, in time,
become all that He wanted it to be.

Meanwhile, my teaching at a large, residential
discipleship ministry was bearing good fruit. I
had taught there for many years and was re-
spected and affirmed. I loved my work and believed in its value.

Although all my students were men, I was confident that I was too strong, too mature and too
spiritual to be tempted to be unfaithful to God or
my husband. I had learned to maintain physical
and psychological distance from them by dressing
modestly and behaving professionally. I wanted
to be an effective teacher, not a distraction.

This had been relatively easy to accomplish in
the classroom, dealing with large groups. But
when I was given an intern to train one-on-one, I
was in for a surprise.

The intern and I shared an office and worked
well together. His hunger for God and his grasp
of the Word greatly touched me. In turn, he expressed to me how deeply my love for the Lord
ministered to his spirit, which was something I
had longed for years to hear from my husband,
but hadn't.

We found it very easy to be open with one another about the personal side of our lives—the
dreams, the disappointments of the past and our

love for God. We understood each other so well that it seemed as though we could read each other's mind at times! We took every possible opportunity to study together and encourage one another. The knitting of our spirits grew daily.

Just seeing his smile each morning made the world light up for me. I was happier than I could remember ever having been in my life. I felt more keenly alive, more sensitive and more creative, and I taught with more passion than ever. Although I had never been able to compose music before, during this time I wrote 16 songs!

It was as though I had been emotionally reborn—this time free of insecurities and the pain of rejection. I was loved for ME—just as I was! It seemed like a gift from God! Someone believed in me, was delighted at watching my life and cared what I thought and felt.

My life became split. I became split. There was life at the ministry with him, where I was appreciated and understood; and there was life at home, where I felt that I never measured up. My husband became a stranger to me. I slowly lost the vision for a richer marriage. The hope that had sustained me died.

I began to imagine life free of my husband. Of course, I had no intention of leaving him; I was just "imagining." I was on the very brink of the chasm—a lamb with one foot over the ledge.

My authorities at the ministry warned me directly and indirectly many times not to spend so much time with the intern. But I thought that I could handle myself and that they were being nar-row-minded. To abandon such joy was unthink-able! I was going to prove that I could be best friends with someone who wasn't my husband and not commit sin.

𝒯urning Point

Then one day John Sandford's book *Why Some Christians Commit Adultery*, came into my hands and I began to read. It opens with a description of spiritual adultery, the unintentional entering into one another's hearts that easily occurs between trusting people who spend time together, espe-cially in ministry.

As I continued to read, something snapped in-side me. I knew that I had to hear from God. Something wasn't right. I asked for the afternoon off and headed for a public park in the next town.

All the way there in the car, I begged God to show me my heart. In response, the phrase "slime pit" kept pressing in on my senses. I tried to see and hear something else—anything else—but to no avail.

And then as I spent hours walking the foot-paths in the park, God brought back to me mem-ory after memory of the times I had denied Him, abused my leadership position in the ministry, be-trayed trust and become a law unto myself.

Finally, face down on the ground beside the path there in the park, I cried out to God for mercy. My heart broke as I saw my darkness, and I repented of what He had shown me.

He met me there, and I knew I was forgiven. But it was just the beginning, for I had much to learn. The long process of cleansing would take years and would prove to be full of pain, but also of great promise for my life.

God started teaching me, step by step as I could bear it, deeper matters regarding love and the sanctity of my spirit.

In the months to come, when I found myself unable to sleep at night, I sat cross-legged in the middle of our living room floor and poured over my Bible, searching to understand myself and what had happened. On one such night, I stumbled upon Malachi 2:14-16:

> The LORD is acting as the witness between you and the wife (husband) of your youth, because you have broken faith with her (him), though she (he) is your partner, the wife (husband) of your marriage covenant.
>
> Has not the LORD made them one? In flesh and spirit they are his. And why one? Because he was seeking godly offspring. So guard yourself in your spirit, and do not break faith with the wife (husband) of your youth.

I was pierced through! For the first time, I had a revelation of how serious God was about covenant. It didn't matter in the slightest how happy I was with my husband. At all costs, I was to "guard my spirit" and not break faith with him. I had sinned on both counts.

More profoundly, I had broken faith with God. He had told me to trust Him in all things and not to have any other gods in my life. I had made an idol out of "being loved." I had broken God's heart by looking to someone else to meet my needs. I had forgotten that I was indeed His Bride, too, married to Him forever! He had been loving me dearly all the time, but I had not learned to draw from that love.

The intern suffered immeasurably as a new Christian because I had allowed him to look to me instead of God for deep friendship and love. I had sinned in thinking I had the right to be anything special to him. I failed miserably in my greatest task—to point him constantly to God. I let him look at and to me, and even became possessive of his attention. I acted out of selfishness. Satan had spotted the wounds and the spiritual pride in my heart, baited the trap and lured me into a relationship that was based on thievery and unfaithfulness. What easy prey I had been for him!

For more than a year after that, the Lord washed me over and over again, with my own tears. I learned at His feet as I wept. His great mercy, love and forgiveness were there as each lesson was burned into my heart. And He never let me out of His arms as He disciplined me.

In the midst of the most difficult times, the Lord reminded me of something I had forgotten: Nine months before I ever met the intern, I had prayed that God would send His Refiner's Fire into my life. I had earnestly petitioned Him to expose and burn up anything in my heart that could come between Him and me. God had simply answered that prayer! As I embraced the Fire, I began to sense His holiness as never before, and to learn how thoroughly I am to worship my God with my very life.

Time has passed, but it still takes very little to remind me of the sorrow that comes from trying to rewrite His law, or from thinking I have discovered some new freedom.

I am reminded of something I wrote many years ago:

> Strange, how easily we choose Death
> Even while soundly breathing.
> And if that Dying seems of our own
>   creation,
> Pride fools us into thinking of it
>   As New Life,
> And Sin tells us it is
> A fresh, original Freedom.
> Then we find ourselves in Ancient Chains.

It is easy to open our personal spirits to someone else who loves the Lord we love. But when the relationship becomes exclusive or indispensable to us, we know that it has become a matter of worship.

While seemingly glorious, life becomes blurred and out of focus as the rebellion spreads. As we fight God for control, we lose touch with reality, and our ability to discern ceases. We have pulled another, who is not our God nor our mate, into the deepest part of our lives. The unfaithfulness is lodged in our very spirits!

Because it is not sexual, we are not on guard against it. But spiritual adultery is fully as dangerous. It slowly eats away at our relationships with God and others, inevitably destroying intimacy and trust. It poisons and blinds our spirits inch by inch, setting the stage for sexual adultery.

Who Is in Danger

Candidates for spiritual adultery are typically sincere, committed and spiritually sensitive people who would be appalled at the thought of ever being unfaithful to God or their spouses.

But they usually share a common misconception: that human love can rescue them from their weaknesses and failures, hurts and sorrows, and that human love is their inalienable right. They haven't fully grasped the literal way in which Jesus can meet their needs and more than compensate for the lack of love from others. Whatever joy they find in that other person is but a counterfeit of what is in Jesus. Without realizing it, they have judged His love insufficient.

The truth is that His love is perfect all the time! It is always there, always fully capable of making us truly happy! It isn't based on our performance, and it never pulls back.

- It is His love that makes us full enough to be sensitive and faithful to a spouse who just cannot seem to love us very well, or who has great difficulty understanding our needs.

- It is His love that prevents bitterness and brings humility upon us as we choose to esteem the other more highly.

- It is His love that reminds us that, but for His grace, we would be destined for hell. We are not qualified to sit in judgment of our spouses. It is not our job—only God's, and He is merciful!

- It is His love that enables us to see our own offenses and say we're sorry, without fear of losing our value. It is by identifying with Him that we are able to forgive and become of no reputation, laying down our self-interest for the sake of the other's well-being.

We learn this freedom by *knowing* Jesus and letting His love heal our broken hearts, so that we will not be susceptible to such sin again.

It is safe to be transparent and simple with Him. He loves His little lambs! We must unashamedly look straight into His face and say with confidence, "I know You will take care of me. Cleanse me and heal me. I need You! Help me grow up!"

Renewed Marriage

During the months that followed my repentance, my husband and I were greatly helped through Christian counseling. We slowly discov-

ered and dealt with the root problems and judgments within each of our hearts that had set the
stage for spiritual adultery.

It has taken a long, long time, but we have finally become good friends—friends who can tell
the truth and accept it from each other, and who
are considerate of one another. We greatly value
each other's life before God and man. We have
brand-new respect for one another, out of which
is growing a faithful love.

You know, any of us could have loved and married someone else and have been happy. But we
didn't. We married—for whatever reasons—the
one we did, and now it's God's will that we come to
maturity together. Wishing things were different,
or that we had married someone else, throws us
into the lap of deception. Then we play the fool.

We must value our spouses and learn to understand each other. Counseling is critical, because it
allows someone who is objective to hold up a
mirror to our blind spots. We usually refuse to be
open and to deal with our offenses, weaknesses
and wounds until we allow someone outside the
situation to hold us accountable.

Feelings of powerlessness and inferiority, loneliness and rejection, poor communication, an excessive desire for attention, anger, jealousy,
fantasizing and ungratefulness must be brought
out and resolved. We need to forgive, repent, be
cleansed and healed.

If you have connected deeply with someone
else, ask God to dissolve all spiritual and emo-

tional ties with that other person. Renounce all pledges you ever made to that person and ask God to totally take away any vestiges of unseemly love or affection that might still be in you.

After separating yourself from the person spiritually, you should separate physically. The person must be dead to you! Continuing to work together or have any other regular contact is out of the question, if you want to be totally free. It is often necessary to change churches, move into a different ministry or even leave the area. Once you have been allowed into another's heart, the pathway back in is too well worn and comforting not to be traveled again at a glance or a word. We are not emotionless machines; it is cruel to test and tempt ourselves so.

For a time after you have separated from the person, thoughts and longings for that person usually return, even though you have repented. When they do, take them captive and give up ownership of them to God. Use the temptation as an opportunity to thank God for saving you from a worse fate, and recommit yourself to faithfulness to God and your family.

If it is your mate who falls into spiritual adultery, ask yourself what insensitivity on your part might have contributed to it. You may need to do some soul searching and repenting of your own. Start talking with and truly listening to your spouse, and you will likely learn some new things about yourselves!

Don't delay—swallow your pride and get help for your marriage before it is too late. You and your mate are more important than any ministry, and if leaving the ministry will facilitate healing, do it.

As leaders, teachers, staff members—whatever our ministry—we must have our lives in order. Whatever seeds of selfishness or imbalance we allow into our private lives will be sown alongside the good seed of the Word we minister. Every part of the kingdom of self must be torn down to produce an undefiled life message that is safe to give to others.

Illegal bonding, spirit to spirit, adulterates (pollutes) our lives, marriages and ministries. It destroys discernment and twists reality. We must guard our hearts at any cost. It is time to take responsibility and grow up! Spiritual adultery is a deadly deception; no one involved in it escapes unscathed.

> *Lord, keep me from giving my glory away.*
> *Guard me from false loves and show me*
>   *Your way*
> *And I will fly free on eagle's wings,*
>   *And true peace will be upon me,*
>   *And true peace will be upon me!*

If we don't repent and flee the person and the situation, we can expect:

- to commit sexual adultery eventually
- to lose everything we hold dear

- to wake up one day to see that this "love" that made our hearts sing has turned common and stale in our grasp
- to discover that the same longings that caused all our losses still rage within our soul
- to hear the familiar strains of the Pied Piper's song for what they are: mocking echoes from the pit of hell.

LAMBS, BEWARE!

WALKING SAFELY ON THE LEDGE

The prudent see danger and take refuge,
  but the simple keep going and suffer for it.
    (Proverbs 27:12)

He who conceals his sins does not prosper,
  but whoever confesses and
    renounces them finds mercy.
      (Proverbs 28:13)

  . . .the tongue of the wise brings healing.
    (Proverbs 12:18)

Whoever gives heed to instruction prospers,
  and blessed is he who trusts in the Lord.
    (Proverbs 16:20)

Chapter 5

TAKING COUNSEL

*He had stumbled and fallen, tumbling onto his back
in the dry grass near the pasture's edge. After having
struggled for hours to right himself, the foundered lamb
lay still, resigned to the slow death to come.*

*Then with what little energy remained, he sum-
moned one last desperate "baa" for help. The Shepherd,
at that moment passing nearby, heard him! In an instant, He was beside the dusty lamb, heaving him onto
his side and then to his feet.*

"You're nothin' but a no-good punk! Get out of
my sight! I never want to see your face around
here again!"

Rage pulsed through every cell of Mark's body.
One move by that kid, and his fist would smash
into the boy's freckled face.

Tim didn't say a word, nor did he so much as

shuffle his feet. He was stunned, pierced through by the angry words screamed at him by his youth pastor. There was no point in defending himself or his friends. Mark was irrational and dangerous. It was not just that the rage far outweighed the offense. Something deeper was going on, and it was scary.

Their relationship would never be the same. Mark's repeated challenge to the youth during many previous months—"Win your schools for Christ!"—echoed absurdly in Tim's mind. Such a noble pursuit seemed irrelevant and foreign now, like something from another planet. Tim, like others in the youth group who had seen this side of Mark, withdrew and closed himself in. Recovery seemed distant.

The next day, Mark couldn't recall the words he had hurled at Tim the night before. He just felt trapped, doomed to a pattern of anger that had started many years before.

As the day wore on, justification set in, and the inner demand to be a "champion" won out. Admission of guilt would be weakness, and that was out of the question.

＊   ＊   ＊

Our behavior is our responsibility. But what do we do if we find ourselves repeatedly trapped in the same paralyzing responses? What if a certain behavior by someone else always throws us into fits of anger or sieges of bitterness, despite our best intentions to respond in love? What if peace in the ministry workplace is always just beyond reach but rejection upon us at every turn?

Counseling and inner healing can be of great help to us in coming to peaceful terms with our pasts, applying the cross in repentance or forgiveness. We are like trees, with roots that go down into our parents' lives, and the shape of our trunks reflect the nurturing—or lack thereof—we received in childhood. We spread our branches in adulthood as a direct reaction to how we perceive ourselves, and our self-perception is based on the influence of others, especially during our adolescence. Whether our fruit is sweet or sour, fully developed or stunted indicates the degree of soundness in our lives. Counselors that are gifted by God and trained in the Word can be mightily used to help us trace our weaknesses to their sources and apply the Lord's healing power and forgiveness in discerning prayer.

When we accept Jesus as Savior, He brings our spirits to life. We are newly born of the Holy Spirit, adopted by the Father and heirs with Jesus of all the promises. So begins the journey of transformation to become what God had always intended us to be.

At the point of salvation, many of our sorrows are immediately healed as we accept God's forgiveness of our sins. Our hearts are washed by the blood of the Lamb. The power of sin is broken, and we now have the ability to forsake evil.

But many well-worn paths of selfishness and artful dodging, to avoid the painful breaking of our stubborn wills, are still clearly defined and all too familiar. As hard as we might try, we find ourselves ducking down those old paths to escape the cross being applied to our flesh-life. While our spirits detect the ways of God, our souls still cling to this earth. Even though we have sent a great taproot into the Father's heart and are learning to draw life from Him, many old and twisted roots are still connected to long-past judgments and woundings.

Our thought lives need to be renewed by the washing of the Word, our wills broken through discipline and correction, and our emotions healed by Jesus and brought into balance. All of creation—including us—groans for total deliverance and the maturity of the saints. We sometimes long for heaven, so that our perfecting will be accomplished in one mighty act of transformation, but that is not God's way with us.

However, Jesus, through the cross and the shedding of His powerful blood, gives us the capacity for wholeness now. His Kingdom has come, and we are to pray that His will be done now on earth as it is in heaven. I am impressed that the Apostle Paul, in Second Corinthians five, directs us to be reconciled to God, and then appoints us as ministers of reconciliation of our fellowmen to God. Therein lies not only the role of the preacher, evangelist and teacher, but also of the counselor, advisor and godly friend.

The astounding thing about the Body of Christ is that it is *a body*; it is meant to function as a unit, not as individual, "Lone Ranger" parts. We are foolish and disobedient to remain isolated from those God has gifted to come alongside us and hold up mirrors to our blind spots. While we must choose wisely the persons to whom we open up our lives for counseling, we must not neglect this accountability and exposure.

At any given time, there are others in the Body who have learned lessons ahead of us and have been placed near us for a reason. They can assist us in applying the same lessons to our lives. Only pride deceives us into thinking that we must be self-sufficient. The truth is that we can't afford to be!

No matter how pronounced or obscure our role is in the ministry, we all need to be known well by someone who will tell us the truth, and draw us up short when necessary. Rare is the friend who can always do this; it is sometimes better that we also be held accountable by someone whom we see as an advisor or counselor. The relationship should be one of trust and confidentiality, for sometimes painful corrections to our lives are needed and must be made with discretion and thoroughness. We must drop all thoughts of impressing them right from the beginning, or we will not tell the truth when conditions are most critical and potentially embarrassing.

A search for the faulty structures in our lives can be very helpful in understanding the dilemmas we fall into—particularly in relationships. Spiritually discerning counselors or advisors, guided by the Holy Spirit, can help us bring to the cross all the bitter roots, injuries and injustices of the past, as the Holy Spirit convicts us of unhealthy motives for present behavior. They can assist us in prayer to come to an accurate view of God's character and what He means to be to us throughout life. They can pronounce deliverance to us when necessary and cheer us on as we forge new trails of godly responses to circumstances and others' behavior.

Some things are learned only through failure; being counseled and held accountable will not prevent every error. Indeed, stubbornness in particular rarely yields until bludgeoned to death. However, when the very hand of God has fallen to mercifully break our outer man, a counselor can assist us in reaping from the experience all that God intended us to learn. A faithful counselor will also keep us from rationalizing, justifying and retreating in self-pity. It is another form of being held accountable—this time to learn our lesson thoroughly.

We must grow up. We must stop failing one another and disillusioning those who look to us for help in finding God. So much more productivity could come from our lives if we would take more seriously our own weaknesses and need to be ministered unto by others in the Body. It is only common sense to avail ourselves of every protection and provision available within the Body of Christ.

When we become vulnerable to others' counsel, we may be amazed at the insight they have to offer. They have learned, as we must also, that God gives us difficult experiences for two reasons: to cause us to cast ourselves upon Him in repentance, forgiving those who have hurt us, and to teach others to do the same.

Everyone must submit himself to the governing authorities, for there is no authority except that which God has established. The authorities that exist have been established by God. Consequently, he who rebels against the authority is rebelling against what God has instituted, and those who do so will bring judgment on themselves. . . . For [the one in authority] is God's servant to do you good. But if you do wrong, be afraid, for he does not bear the sword for nothing. He is God's servant, an agent of wrath to bring punishment on the wrongdoer. Therefore, it is necessary to submit to the authorities, not only because of possible punishment but also because of conscience. (Romans 13:1-2, 4-5)

Chapter 6

TRUSTING GOD: STAYING UNDER AUTHORITY

Settled securely by the fresh, cool stream that wound lazily through the tall grass on the southern side of the ledge, the lambs lay sleeping.

One awoke. Then another. Something was different. Looking around anxiously for the Shepherd, the two were startled to see his mat empty. They had been trained to stay by the stream, but fear had them confused.

Soon all the sheep were awake, and panic broke out among the flock.

Rare is the ministry which has not gone through grim times because of un-Christlike or unethical behavior by one or several of its leaders.

In spite of 2,000 years of Church experience, we still wrestle within our hearts to determine what to do when those over us need correction. Are we responsible to force them to change? Can we submit to them and still serve effectively in the ministry?

When a leader becomes a law unto himself and begins to justify practices that conflict with God's principles, those under him feel the pain first. The grief runs deep; the helplessness, frustration and anger can be overwhelming.

In such situations, it is as though the leader forgets that each staff or church member is as knit to the ministry as he is, and each is tremendously affected by the attitudes and practices he demonstrates. There is something in the nature of deception that causes the leader to imagine himself to be operating in isolation, as well as by a different "book of rules." He becomes disconnected from those under him before he realizes it.

Jesus taught, in Matthew 18:15-17, to go to someone who is in error, appealing our case honestly and without malice. If he doesn't listen, we are to take witnesses with us and appeal again. If he still refuses to repent and change his behavior, he is to be taken before church leaders.

Fortunately, more and more churches have developed plans for handling such cases and exercising correction and discipline. Accountability *before* problems develop has become of greater concern, and Christian counseling for pastors is becoming more acceptable. Although we have a long way to go, perhaps someday we will *prevent* more pain for everyone than we have in the past had to endure.

But in many a parachurch ministry, the leader is not under the consistent authority and covering of a home church. He must frequently spend Sunday mornings and evenings speaking to other churches on behalf of the ministry. His "home" church and pastor rarely see him, except when he speaks there as well. He confides in a personal way with few people, if any, who could help him. In such cases, only the board of directors of the ministry or of the denomination—if the ministry is under a denomination—can possibly act to effect change.

Unfortunately, rarely do board members work closely enough on site with the leader to be able to fully appreciate the stress staff members might be under. They are usually the last to know when there are deep problems in the ministry. Their power may also be more in theory than in fact.

Because staff members are usually hesitant to step out in what may appear to be defiance or insubordination, they are inclined to repress their misgivings, hoping and praying that the leader will wake up and change of his own accord. Those who know how to release the offenses to God in forgiveness are able to serve effectively in spite of it, at least while the leader is not committing moral sin. Those who allow the offenses to penetrate their spirits, yielding to anger and unforgiveness, grow petulant and bitter.

The first group wait a long time before they appeal; the latter group are in no shape to appeal because of the bitterness in their own hearts. So, for these two reasons, often the leader is given a great deal of grace.

Personal Example

Several years ago, I watched the procedure of appeal carried out in a large ministry where I was a teacher. After concerted prayer over a period of many months, a concerned staff member began the appeal process. The director refused to respond to the appeal in a positive way. Further appeals brought the same result, and since the need for reform seemed urgent, appeals were written to his superiors in the denomination.

A delegation was sent to hear staff members testify regarding conditions in the ministry and the practices of the director. Excitement, tinged with apprehension, swept through the ministry that day as staff members lined up to take their turns to speak with board members. Hope ran high that action would finally be taken for the ministry's sake, as well as the director's.

After a few weeks of suspense, things began to happen—but not as we expected. Amazingly, the director emerged with more power than ever, and several men, including the writer of the appeal, were unceremoniously fired! A few others resigned quietly and left in dismay and disbelief. Many of those who remained served from that day on in fear.

There was an eerie speechlessness among those who remained. What had happened? What were we to learn from this? It had seemed so logical to challenge authority. With things going wrong in the ranks above us, shouldn't we use whatever power we have to right the wrong? Surely God would be in it, breathing a sigh of relief that someone was finally taking action! Had we gone too far? Had any of us acted out of self-right-eousness or a condemning spirit?

What about the free will of the director? Was it simply a matter of his exercising his freedom of choice against a just appeal, and not a sin on our part?

Each staff member in the months ahead had to sort it all out individually, according to what was in his own heart. The men who had been fired not only had to sort it out and come to peace, but had to struggle to find new employment and, in some cases, sell their homes and move. It was a terribly difficult time.

Although I had not testified and was still there, my heart was very much in turmoil over what had happened. I knew God had a lesson in it for me as well.

One day a few weeks later, I was quizzing a re-medial student for an upcoming test. I will never forget the questions I had to ask him and the an-swers he gave.

Question: Who judges sin?
Answer: God.

Question: Why does He sometimes take so long?
Answer: Because of His mercy.

I abruptly left the student standing there and fled to my office, pierced through by this forgotten facet of God's love. I wept as I realized in that moment that my heart had had no mercy whatsoever as I had commiserated with other staff about the problems in the ministry. I had personally done nothing to try to reach the director or the unbroken men with whom he had unwisely surrounded himself. I had kept my distance and had sacrificed nothing to help.

That God allowed the director more time to repent on his own was due to His mercy, not His helplessness in the situation. As for any of us, God's mercy would bring resolution in time.

In God's Time

I sensed God telling me to "take a break" from this ministry for a while as He continued to work in the situation. I left and taught in a Christian school for two years.

Many things happened back at the ministry in the next year. The unethical practices continued. Then, within a relatively short period of time, the director and two of his inner circle contracted serious diseases and died! One other left with the receptionist, and the last one went back to drugs and the streets.

Before the director died, he made peace with

many people, but it was a sad, sad ending to a mighty preacher's life. I remember now the great, convicting sermons he had preached and the mercy he had often shown to some very unworthy vessels.

I love him now and wish I could have gotten past his gruff exterior and encouraged him in the Lord. It tears at my heart. He had been God's anointed to teach us to trust God, not man. God was forever faithful to him, and they are now together in glory.

So much came alive to me through all the suffering! I learned some important lessons about trusting God while remaining under man's authority:

- My authorities are ordained by God.
- My job is to work faithfully and respectfully for him as unto the Lord, keeping my own life pure.
- I am to pray earnestly for him each day.
- When something done by my authority is wrong, I must first deal with my own attitude, and then make an appeal with a forgiving spirit.
- I must not allow myself to be intimidated; we are all in this together, and we need each other.
- My leaders are my brothers and my sisters. I am to speak the truth in love while esteeming them above myself, and then leave the results to God.
- Discerning right from wrong is wise, but judging my authorities is God's job, not

mine. Judging my authorities may reveal spiritual pride in my heart, as well as ignorance; rarely does one person know the whole story.

- Judging my authorities gives birth to gossip, slander and bitterness, and reveals a great lack of trust in God's power and ability to deal with His servants.

- If the situation becomes oppressive or I am asked to sin, God will give the release to leave. At that point, my exit should be made quietly, without passing my grievances on to others inside or outside the ministry.

In any conflict within a church or parachurch ministry, God deals with each participant individually. His purposes are as varied as the people affected, for we are each at a different place in our growth. Each of us has something to learn, tailormade for our weaknesses.

The person who has forgiven and feels free of judgment can make a proper appeal for change when a situation is bad. But the guilty party may not respond as he should, for reasons we may never know. The appealer must be prepared to suffer reprisals without becoming bitter. He must count the cost as he is obedient in confronting sin.

Those who watch must remember the mercy God has afforded them and be willing to extend the same to the offender, if God is delaying judgment.

All of us must search our hearts for unhealthy insecurities, resentments born out of jealousy,

fear of man, aptness to believe the worst of others
and self-righteousness. God is as interested in
dealing with these in us as He is in straightening
out our leaders.

When David was hiding in the deserts and hills
with his band of debtors and discontents, he
twice had opportunity to kill King Saul, the man
who was madly stalking his life. He had previously appealed to Saul to be reasonable and not
fear him, but Saul had not relented, and now the
power was in David's hands. His own men urged
him to do Saul in once and for all in order to end
their own miserable exile.

The first time, David cut off a corner of Saul's
robe while he lay sleeping, and felt guilty for doing
even that. The second time, he emphatically said,
"Don't destroy him! Who can lay a hand on the
LORD's anointed and be guiltless?" (1 Samuel 26:9).
He went on to say that God would take care of the
matter in His own way.

Even though Saul had violently hurled spears
at him on three occasions, David refused to respond by spear-throwing in return. Jesus Himself gives substance to David's behavior when
He tells us to bless when cursed, and return
good for evil. He lays out the pattern of appeal
in Matthew 18:15-17, and then says to simply
cease fellowship with the offender if he doesn't
respond.

Throughout the process, we are to forgive as
we have been forgiven. Hebrews 12:15 further
says that we must "See to it that no one misses

the grace of God and that no bitter root grows up to cause trouble and defile many."

Ultimately, our trust must be in God. He is the great Judge of the earth, yet we may be surprised at the measure of His mercy. After all, He saved us! Underneath all our passion for justice and our defense of God's name, this must be remembered. It will hold us steady when we don't understand why God takes so long in judging sin. Remembering it will put God on the throne, yielding Him the ultimate rule of the world. We must trust Him to take care of the most grievous of situations. He will!

The Good Shepherd is not worried about His own reputation. He is concerned that we learn to trust Him when there is no sign of relief—when all the grass on The Ledge turns brown and tasteless. God *will* remember His sheep and bring the rain . . . just in time.

A good name is more desirable
  than great riches;
to be esteemed is better than silver or gold.
      (Proverbs 22:1)

Kings take pleasure in honest lips;
  they value a man who speaks the truth.
      (Proverbs 16:13)

The LORD detests lying lips,
  but he delights in men who are truthful.
      (Proverbs 12:22)

Surely you desire truth in the inner parts; you teach me wisdom in the inmost place. (Psalm 51:6)

When a man makes a vow to the LORD or takes an oath to obligate himself by a pledge, he must not

break his word but must do everything he said.
(Numbers 30:2)

But I tell you that men will have to give account on the day of judgment for every careless word they have spoken. (Matthew 12:36)

The fear of the LORD teaches a man wisdom,
 and humility comes before honor.
  (Proverbs 15:33)

Chapter 7

A GOOD NAME: KEEPING YOUR WORD

One lamb was missing! The Shepherd ranged quickly but thoroughly over the pasture where they had been the night before. He remembered the song He sang to the sheep before the sky grew dark and they had fallen to sleep. It spoke of promises, of faithfulness and love that kept its word.

"I'll find you, little lamb, I'll find you," He called over and over, hour after hour as He searched.

Just as the sun rose and fatigue dogged his every step, He found the lamb behind a small rock He had missed in the dark during the night. The reunion was sweet.

MaryBeth waited pensively in the reception area of the large overseas missions office. Her appointment with the director was already 30 minutes overdue, but she could be patient.

She had spent $175 to make this trip, which was a lot of money for her right now. But the director, Reverend Hubbard, had promised to thoroughly review her application for a missions scholarship ahead of time, so that he could be ready with a decision on the trip to Bosnia *today!*

Having spoken with him only over the telephone, she had guessed him to be older than he actually was. Through his slightly ajar office door, she could see him behind the big mahogany desk. His secretary was laughing with him about something.

He's surely going to call me in any minute, she thought to herself as she pushed back the cuff of her jacket to check her watch. Another ten minutes had gone by. More light banter filtered out of the room.

She felt the muscles in her back tighten a little. *Lord, keep me calm and forgiving. Once I get in there, everything will be all right. I've come too great a distance and spent too much money on the trip to give up now just because he's being rude.* The conversation with herself, however, wasn't making her feel much better.

Finally, after more conversation and laughter, the attractive secretary emerged from the office. Seeing MaryBeth, she cleared her throat and called her name.

"Miss Murray, Reverend Hubbard is free now to speak with you."

MaryBeth took a deep breath and walked quickly into the room. She reached across the desk and invited a handshake. He smiled and returned it, and then motioned her to an armchair in front of the desk.

"Ah, yes. Now, what is your name again?"

Surprised that he needed to be told, she blurted out, "MaryBeth Murray!"

He knit his brows in a puzzled look. "Now why have you come to see me?"

Before she could answer, he remembered. "Oh, yes. It was something about a missions trip, wasn't it? Let's see. I vaguely remember something about an application form."

He scratched his head and then began rummaging through the deep side drawers of his desk. "It's here somewhere. Now where did I put it?"

Finally, he dug it out of the bottom drawer. It was still in the envelope in which she had sent it . . . unopened.

"Oh, my goodness! I forgot all about it. Now what was it that you had wanted?"

Before she could even muster a response he continued, "We're so busy around here. You know, what with all the fund raising we have to do, remodeling our offices and making connections in the community, I've really not had time to look at your application. I'm sure you can appreciate that."

MaryBeth's heart cried out silently to God. *Don't let me get bitter. I know I'm just an unknown sitting here in a very important man's office.*

But I'm feeling worthless and angry. Please help me surrender my frustration so I can know Your will.

* * *

Satan's agents, Pride and Arrogance, stalk us relentlessly and all too often overtake us. How companionable many of us are with these enemies in the area of keeping our word!

It's no surprise that Satan would design the destruction of our credibility. If our own word becomes suspect, so also will God's Word when spoken by us. It's an ingenious plan. But how simply it's carried out!

This destruction begins in the little things: telling someone that we will get back to them with an answer by a certain time, and then not bothering to do so; not showing up to meetings or appointments on time; not returning a borrowed item when promised; not paying a fellow believer for a service in the amount agreed upon because we changed our minds.

And it goes on to bigger offenses: not paying staff in full when money is tight, but continuing some other ministry project instead; inviting a speaker who must travel some distance and then offering him nothing for his labor, not even travel expenses; not paying bills until we are tracked down and threatened; arriving late at speaking engagements (often breaking every speeding law to get there); claiming more converts or higher "cure rates" than is accurate in order to induce people to support us. The list could go on and on.

It is heartbreaking that in many ministries, the staff have jokes about how unreliable everyone is. If the unsaved could hear the stories we pass among ourselves about the selfish and presumptuous treatment ministry workers inflict upon one another, they would hardly risk trusting our Lord. The problem rests in the fact that the stories are often true.

What lies behind our irresponsible behavior? What are the tragic character flaws that seek to rewrite the laws of love? What is at the heart of all arrogance, pride, and the disregard or neglect of others? What and who is on the throne of our lives at those times?

They are vain imaginations of our own importance that manifest themselves as we lower the other man to beg at our feet, unworthy in our eyes of honest treatment. How soon we forget Calvary and the reason for His pain—*our* unworthiness, not the other guy's. We never, no matter how long we have been a believer, are removed from being the recipient of His salvation and grace and from being the reason for his suffering.

We can never attain the status of savior of the world, writer of the law, enforcer of a new system of justice. We are only forever indebted to Jesus and forever a servant of our brothers, never their lord, never exempt from the rules of decent behavior. If we plead that we were just never taught the rules and therein lies our difficulty, then by all means, we must learn them and learn them fast!

Let us listen carefully to each promise or commitment that proceeds from our mouths and give it authenticity by faithfully doing exactly as we have said we would. If we are unable to organize our days so we can carry out our word, then we must repent, apologize and learn to weigh our words as precious jewels. We must utter only those words for which we will hold ourselves accountable.

Within this, the Savior ascends the throne, and we relinquish the scepter to Him. We then lay down the stress and arrogance of human rule and peacefully join the ranks of our fellowman, on our knees in service.

The watching world will take note. " These are men and women of their word. They are faithful and true! Therefore, their Word—their Lord— can be believed and trusted."

The ridicule of the world will be replaced by admiration, and the old stories among the brethren will be replaced by words of gratitude and praise for one another. We will all stretch to embrace the dignity of God.

And the wolves will slink away in the night.

Satan rose up against Israel and incited David to take a census of Israel. . . .

This command was also evil in the sight of God; so he punished Israel. Then David said to God, "I have sinned greatly by doing this. Now, I beg you, take away the guilt of your servant. I have done a very foolish thing.". . .

Then the angel of the LORD ordered Gad to tell David to go up and build an altar to the LORD on the threshing floor of Araunah the Jebusite. . . .

David said to him, "Let me have the site of your threshing floor so I can build an altar to the Lord, that the plague on the people may be stopped. Sell it to me at the full price."

Araunah said to David, "Take it! Let my lord the king do whatever pleases him. Look, I will give the oxen for the burnt offerings, the threshing sledges for the wood, and the wheat for the grain offering. I will give all this."

But King David replied to Araunah, "No, I insist on paying the full price. I will not take for the Lord what is yours, or sacrifice a burnt offering that costs me nothing." (1 Chronicles 21:1, 7-8, 18, 22-24, author's emphasis)

Chapter 8

EMBRACING DISCIPLINE

The stubbornness eased slowly out of the renegade lamb as the days wore on and the Shepherd continued to carry him in his arms. He had repeatedly wandered off, and the Shepherd had had to break his leg to teach him a lesson.

But as it healed, the heartbeat of the Shepherd became like a song to him, changing his own heart as he listened to it day after day. He felt the weariness in the Shepherd's arms, so tired from carrying him.

He also felt the love, and that love moved him deeply. He was glad now for the sore leg. He had learned so much.

When my children were young and misbehaved, I knew that the spanking had to be just right—not too little or they would not understand the seriousness of disobedience, and not too much or they would only see my anger and fear me. The focus had to be right and the discipline thorough. If they knew they had been very bad and I had not disciplined them, they would have been uncomfortable and unhappy, left with their guilt and unsure that I cared.

As men and women in ministry, how do we react when our sins are disclosed and we face discipline? Do we try to escape the price?

Solomon is held to be the wisest man who ever lived, but David displayed a stroke of unparalleled genius in First Chronicles 21:24 when he refused to offer a sacrifice for his sin that cost him nothing. He longed for thorough discipline. He understood the gravity of disobedience and wanted to feel the cost, so he wouldn't do it again.

We are very shortsighted and foolish to desire as little punishment or discipline as possible after disobeying. We must learn how much sin hurts and grieve the losses it brings. If we have not wept and embraced the bruising, perhaps we have not understood what we have done. We are God's children, and He knows how to handle us exactly as we each need. He never makes wrong calls or gives inappropriate discipline, and through His forgiveness, we are set again on our way.

Unfortunately, when we "adults" sin and face discipline, we tend to do either of two things: decide for ourselves how much discipline is necessary; or find ourselves quite virtuous, because our accuser's sins are so much worse in our eyes. Issues become convoluted; guilt and discipline, relative. Faith in a just God, the righteous Judge of the earth, gets lost in the shuffle to protect our reputations—and sometimes our earthly wealth.

＊　＊　＊

Reverend John McMaster is facing a lawsuit right now. His waking and sleeping hours have been haunted by it for the many months since charges were filed. He can't believe that this is happening to him.

A few years ago, he appointed to the position of youth pastor a young man who then molested some of the teens. At the time of the appointment, John was warned that this man had recently been fired from another ministry where he had been suspected of inappropriate sexual behavior. His integrity was truly in question. But the pastor wanted to give him a chance.

The decision backfired. Many people were hurt, and bitterness has taken root within the church. One of the families wants him to pay for what has happened.

Where should he focus? On the sins of the others in not forgiving him? On their error in taking him—a fellow believer—to court over it? On all the good he has done throughout his life, in contrast to this offense?

Or should he forget all else and see only the terrible suffering that could have been avoided if he had taken counsel on the decision back then?

Should he allow himself to feel the pain of the molested, and then cry out in sorrow for that pain—in front of everyone? Should he tell them all that he had been wrong, dreadfully wrong, and ask the church to please forgive him? Should he search his heart for any trace of pride that might have been in him at the time and then confess it as sin before his accusers? What if he were to willingly *offer* all his material possessions as small recompence for their losses and grief? What might happen?

It is likely that massive relief would flow through that local Body, forgiveness slowly replacing the bitterness in their hearts. Faith could be restored that there are yet humble men of God on this earth! Vengeance might be spent, for the scales would be balanced. Perhaps they have only wanted him to take responsibility, weep with them and help them recover.

Best of all, everyone could learn these mighty lessons:

- It is wisdom to take counsel from others, no matter what one's position is in the church.
- No one is always right.
- Human suffering is of more significance than one's reputation or wealth.
- Taking personal responsibility for our decisions and actions is essential in living the Christian life.

- Repentance and discipline set life straight again.

- Repenting publicly is not the end of the world, but rather the beginning of spiritual integrity.

- When any one of us "comes clean," we can again sleep well at night.

But what if the congregation devoured him instead and took every material thing he owned when he made himself transparent and vulnerable? This could happen. Lessons in forgiveness can be spurned. God's heart and his children's are broken over and over by such inconsistency in the Body of Christ. Free will brings great license, even when the price is injury to everyone.

What are we then to learn?

* * *

It was Wednesday night, and Sarah found herself in church, alone. Her hunger for God's presence was consuming. Nothing else mattered anymore.

After years of trying to be perfect, she no longer cared what people thought of her. Tears flowed unchecked down her cheeks throughout the entire praise and worship time, and the pile of damp tissues mounted higher on the empty chair beside her.

She had confessed everything to the board at the DayBreak Ministry, where she had been a counselor for 14 years. Her brief affair with Troy, the director, was over, and so was her career as a Christian counselor. What had begun as a simple, caring friendship with a lonely man in a miserable marriage had ended where she had never dreamed she would be—in bed with Troy. In horror at what had happened, she repented and brought it to a screeching halt.

The cold, gray words of Ben Chase, president of the board, pounded again at the back of her mind. When she had confessed and repented, he had had only this to say to her:

"Empty your desk, pack up your personal things and be out of here by tomorrow morning.

"And keep it quiet. No one needs to know. Troy has been given a new assignment and will get help. He is a great leader and can't go down over this. Just leave quietly. Sorry."

That was it. Troy was redeemed; she was thrown out. She had pleaded for mercy, but there was none. Shame flooded her face with its heat once again.

She knew God forgave her; forgiving herself was the hard part. Furthermore, being stripped of ministry was a grief that hung like a dead weight about her neck, sapping her energy and draining from her any hope for the future. She felt nameless and forgotten.

The music ended, bringing her back to the present. A stranger—gray-haired and solemn, dressed in worn jeans and a blue denim shirt—advanced slowly to the platform and was introduced. She gathered from the introduction that he had been a pastor until three years ago, when he had lost everything. He didn't explain why; perhaps it wasn't important. Many things weren't really important anymore, Sarah mused.

His name meant nothing to her. However, as he spoke, his soft, intense voice penetrated her heart, grabbing every bit of her attention.

She had to strain to catch some of the words, for he seemed to be somewhere else, and his voice often became painfully quiet.

"You see, it's on the cold and lonely mountainside, buffeted by harsh winds and neglected by valley streams, that the stripped planting of God grows strong and resilient. It's there that the roots go down deep into the Father's heart, in spite of rocks and barren terrain. Exposed to the wind, the tree learns to bend with the blast, yet return upright after the onslaught has passed.

"It's there alone that the choice is made between bitterness and sweetness..."

Sarah's heart locked upon these words, the rest of his message passing without her noticing.

Her weeping continued, never stopping for more than a brief minute from time to time. It was as though the years of trying so hard to be good, and then her foolish attempt to rescue a hurting man through human love, were rushing to escape her life all at the same time. It was as though the gates of her heart had been opened and all the treasures that had been protected there were being carried off by invisible, irresistible hands.

The service was over. The stranger prayed. Then quietly, deliberately, he stepped down and walked over to the corner where she sat weeping alone. He waited until Sarah looked up into his eyes.

Four words. "Stay sweet. Stay sweet," he whispered.

A moment longer, and he strode from the building. She never saw him again.

The years of discipline on the mountainside that followed changed Sarah's life forever. She learned to truly hear God's voice and know his everlasting love for her. Compassion took root, and so did a profound respect for God's ways in a fallen world. She became wise to her own flesh and its hunger to rule in God's place.

And the stanger's words and the power of God kept her safe from bitterness through it all.

"Stay sweet. Stay sweet."

*   *   *

Discipline is a blessing! It cuts away the callouses that form over our consciences from time to time. It restores the sensitive nerve endings with which to feel the difference between right and wrong. Discipline is at the very center of finding again the joy of our salvation.

It should be with immense relief that the flesh is stricken, the pride brought low and vision of our common need restored. It is so hard to play God! It is much, much too complicated and confusing! Ruling the world is not the glorious joy it would seem to be. We could lose our minds doing it.

Engineering the survival of our self-life is exhausting and never worth any of the effort. Furthermore, if encouraged to live, it will turn viciously in upon us and pitch us down when we are least on guard. It is at exact odds with the Eternal Life of Jesus within us.

We must let it go! Cherish the discipline! Grieve over sin. Confess it all, and beg God to turn up the fire and burn us clean!

But when the fire is spent, and we know we have heard His voice, we can lay it to rest. We were being broken, not destroyed. When the discipline is complete, it is time to let God's life course again through our hearts out to others.

Remember your weaknesses and failures. Never forget the sin you are fully capable of committing if left to yourself, and know there may be more lurking within your heart.

But it needn't be frightening. Your remembering, my remembering, will help next time. We will more quickly reel in our flesh before Satan has opportunity to grab hold of it. We will learn! We will come to abide in Him, reckoning ourselves at last dead, only alive to His life within us.

We are together in this. There is *no one* in the flock who is exempt. God shows no partiality; He loves us justly and therefore disciplines us as we each need. Our task is to embrace it vigorously, no matter how it hurts or what it costs.

It is good to be gentle with one another, but not soft. The wounds of a friend are faithful. But then we must wash those wounds with the love that puts the past behind.

Through it all, remember: We are disciplined by God because we are His sons; if we were not, He wouldn't bother. He wants us to grow up undefiled and undefiling, healthy and sane.

Proverbs 3:11-12 says: "My son, do not despise the LORD's discipline and do not resent his rebuke, because the LORD disciplines those he loves, as a father the son he delights in."

We mustn't argue with God regarding His choice of people, circumstances or methods by which the discipline comes. He knows best what will drain the life out of our most potent enemies, self-righteousness and pride.

And if we were to lose a "ministry" altogether in order to accomplish this, we might be surprised to find true ministry in the end, when the trappings have all been removed. We then discover that ministry comes not from some building or organization, reputation or applause, but from deep within our very lives—lives yielded fully to the Master's hand.

So cherish God's mighty concern for you, and when discipline must come, embrace it! Through it, as through nothing else, you will seek and find His love.

And we will experience peace—even while on *the ledge*.

IT AMAZES ME

It amazes me
That You should love me so
That You would die
For my heart that injures You
So often, Lord.

It amazes me
That I should find Your hand
Within my own
In that moment I am loneliest
And then, I am no longer alone.

But then, what shall I do with today?
Is it enough to hold Your hand,
Beg You to stay?

It amazes me
That understanding seems
So far away
And yet I long to live
And know Your cross again.

—JS

Therefore confess your sins to each other and pray for each other so that you may be healed. The prayer of a righteous man is powerful and effective.
(James 5:16)

*Then I acknowledged my sin to you
  and did not cover up my iniquity.
I said, "I will confess
  my transgressions to the LORD"—
and you forgave
  the guilt of my sin.* (Psalm 32:5)

Brothers, if someone is caught in a sin, you who are spiritual should restore him gently. But watch yourself, or you also may be tempted. Carry each other's burdens, and in this way you will fulfill the law of Christ. If anyone thinks he is something when he is nothing, he deceives himself.
(Galatians 6:1-3)

I have given them the glory that you gave me, that they may be one as we are one: I in them and you in me. May they be brought to complete unity to let the world know that you sent me and have loved them even as you have loved me. (John 17:22-23)

Chapter 9

REPENTANCE AND RESTORATION

After the broken leg healed, the disciplined lamb was set again among the flock. He felt awkward and clumsy and hoped they wouldn't leave him behind when his leg ached a little and made running tough.

But it was even better than before! The other sheep seemed to sense the change in his spirit; he was gentler now and not at all obnoxious and cocky as he had been. They waited for him and slept close to him at night when it was cold.

Reverend J. Montgomery couldn't believe it. Kathy had turned on him and told! The affair with his secretary was over, and the board was demanding his immediate resignation.

He was humiliated by the dismissal, but grateful that the board was intent on keeping it quiet. If word of this got out, his name would be dragged through the mud by everyone in town. He wouldn't be able to leave his house without inviting stares and whispers wherever he went.

The board wanted him to get counseling, serious counseling with a team they recommended. He was expected to find a secular job to support himself.

"Twenty years of ministry down the drain over this? Are you kidding?" was his response, incredulous that they would think he could walk away from the ministry.

"Haven't I said I was sorry? Why can't I just take a short leave of absence and then be transferred to our sister church in Minersville? I'm fine! I'll never do it again!"

But his plan hadn't flown with them.

Out of work and near panic, J. Montgomery wrote to friends in a distant state whose church happened to need a pastor. He had spoken there several times before, and the people loved him. They hadn't heard about the mess he was in and, in his estimation, didn't need to hear.

If he could just get into that pulpit, he'd prove his worth and everything would be all right.

* * *

There is a great lovelessness within the Body of Christ. Forever fueling this lovelessness is an ignorance, or a forgetting, of the joy of deep and visible repentance.

The mastermind of this whole production, even within us, the redeemed, is the father of lies who tells us that we don't really need a sinner's repentance anymore. What a hideous deception!

Neglecting the value of ongoing repentance induces atrophy in the Body of Christ. Our beauty and strength waste away before our very eyes. Pride tells us that we have escaped some great inconvenience by sweeping our sins under the rug.

We look into the mirror and think we are still the same. Arrogance causes our vision to lack depth perception. We no longer see the deceitfulness of our own hearts. The stage is set for a mighty fall, the agony of which will echo around the world.

The Loss of Repentance

Men and women saved from off the street— who freely confess their sin and rebellion—are for that moment the most blessed of us all! They stand before us and weep, crying out repentance at the altar, embracing with intense gratitude the Father's forgiveness.

There is finally nothing to hide, nothing to lose but their old wretched lives. How like children they so easily become! How in love with the Lord! How sensible and practical as they surrender vice after vice! They soak up nurturing, identify with those still lost, and sacrifice themselves to spread the good news they themselves have so recently found.

But before long, they settle in, adopt our patterns and apathies and begin the quest for "their place" in the Body. They strive, as we did before them, to be "an adult," stifling the very life of Christ, losing the sweet innocence that comes from childlikeness. Soon pride overtakes them again. There is only a change of clothes and language to disguise the ancient companion of the flesh.

The "older" they get in the Christian life and matters of the church, the more ridiculous, difficult and unimportant it seems to be to rush to the altar in tears, confessing all.

And the loss of freedom and cleanness grows. Less and less often are they washed by repentance and forgiveness, and a crust of self-righteousness begins to build about their hearts, numbing them to the horror of the insidious sins of the heart and mind. They become like us.

Do "spiritual adults" no longer sin? Is that why we think that we never need to be washed in the tears of repentance? Is falling upon one's face at the altar, before everyone, merely the clumsy act of a child?

What a deprived and sorry lot we often are who have become grownups! We miss the best—the joy of confession, the blessed relief of being forgiven, the freeing power of discipline and the love within restoration. We miss being hugged as a returning prodigal and the sweetness of being clean once again.

*   *   *

The dingy, yellowed walls of the narrow hallway smelled of stale cigarette smoke. As Jeannie climbed the last flight of stairs to the third floor, the air became more oppressive. Apprehension began to build in her chest.

"Can this possibly be the right address?" she whispered to herself. "No way can I imagine Ted living in this pitiful place."

In spite of the atmosphere, Jeannie smiled. For a moment, she was back in the classroom that she had shared with Ted, where they both had been teachers in a discipleship ministry a few years before. His laughter had been infectious, his droll sense of humor, delightful. He had been so much fun! His round and rosy-cheeked face had been a joy to greet each day.

The poignancy of his teaching on the need for emotional health had gripped and convicted many a student. He had known from experience the horrors of molestation and rejection and could discern the same wounds in them.

They vied for counseling time with him during the lunch hour and after classes. His office walls were literally covered with postcards and notes from students thanking him and expressing their love for him. For Jeannie, too, he had been a major source of encouragement.

But the smile faded from Jeannie's face as she also remembered that fresh tragedy had struck his life not long ago. He lost his best friend through a heart attack; soon after, his brother died of AIDS. He felt alone. The door of his spirit swung shut in mourning and never really opened again.

No one around him had noticed. More ministry responsibility was heaped upon him, because he never said no. He was always on display—leading, teaching, ministering to others.

A door slammed loudly somewhere in the old building, and Jeannie's thoughts suddenly returned to the present. The musty smell assaulted her once again, and she tried not to breathe too deeply of the oppressive air.

Not knowing for sure which apartment would be his, her attention was caught by a shiny, brass nameplate on one of the doors as she rounded a corner. She strained through the semi-darkness to read it.

THIS RESIDENCE PROTECTED
BY A .357 MAGNUM

Her heart jumped. She quickly moved on to the last door down the hall. Something inside told her that this was Ted's door.

She knocked softly. A slow shuffle of feet across the floor within the room could be heard amid the chattering of the TV talk show.

Very hesitantly, the door was opened about six inches. Yes, it was Ted, but what changes had come over him! His skin was sallow and his eyes empty. His clothing hung upon his frame, for he had lost a great deal of weight. There was no expression whatsoever on his face.

"Who is it?" he intoned wearily.

"Ted, it's me, Jeannie! May I come in?"

After a moment's hesitation, he slowly opened the door enough for her to slip into the room. It was hard to tell, but he seemed glad to see her. He led her into the living room, where they found places to sit amidst the clutter on the couch.

A labored conversation began. But gradually he relaxed and responded more freely, although in distant, weary tones.

Jeannie gathered that he had been let go from the ministry for no longer being effective, and for his dependency upon drugs, especially anti-depressants. He was empty, destitute and bitter.

"Ted, how did it all come to this?" Jeannie gently asked as their eyes met. "What went wrong?"

Ted shifted his gaze to the floor for a long moment. The words came slowly but deliberately.

"I was never able to go to the altar. I was a leader and teacher, an example, someone who had all the answers. I could never get to the altar to cry out my anger to God for the hurts in my life and get prayer from others." He hesitated, then began again.

"I wasn't supposed to have the deep problems I had. I was on a pedestal, and I couldn't get off. I craved the altar but could never find it!" He sighed, then continued.

"The ministry consumed me. There was no time to just have fun or to get away from it. The ministry became my life, then sucked that very life from me." His voice trailed off.

The effort to share with her had left him visibly worn. Jeannie glanced at her watch. It was time for her to leave.

"May I visit you again in a few days? I'll be in town until Friday," she asked as she held his hand to say goodbye.

He slowly nodded his assent.

After the door closed behind her, she hesitated. She could hear again the slow shuffle of his feet amid the chattering of the TV talk show.

It broke her heart.

* * *

There is a great outcry for restoration of fallen leaders, and it is a true word. But no one can be restored until he has lain upon his face before God and come clean before the brethren.

But how can he fall upon his face when the church expects only perfection? Our penchant for hero worship—and many leaders' love of that worship—has created bigger-than-life men who would rather perish than face their own weaknesses. It often takes "an act of God" to dethrone them and restore them to the common fellowship and blessed repentance.

On the other hand, how can the rest of us "undercover sinners" in the church honestly embrace and restore someone who is repenting of the same sins that we hide within our own hearts? Should we compound the hypocrisy by play-acting? Does our own secrecy make it too dangerous to get close to the fallen person for fear of our own exposure?

Are we sometimes more concerned with maintaining an appearance of purity than in being pure? What a sweet anointing would pour over the land if true repentance were released from out of our proud religious hearts! We're dirty, every one of us, and we desperately need a bath!

Honesty is the beginning of everything. I know from experience that my effectiveness as a teacher has stemmed not from the intelligence of my answers in the classroom but from my transparency. Over the years many students have thanked me for being honest about my own life and for taking risks in exposing my mistakes so that they could learn from them.

I also understand now why there has never been a "generation gap" between my own children and me: We are able to talk honestly about real issues, and none of us has to hide our sins from the other in order to be accepted or loved. Indeed, we are always drawn closer to God and to each other as we apologize and seek forgiveness. This holds a great lesson for us in the church.

Confession and repentance—beginning with the grownups first—should be a normal event. We teach by example. There is no place for hypocrisy and self-righteousness in any family, especially the family of God. Forgiveness, restoration and the healing of all who participate will not be far behind.

The Need for Restoration

While in the ministry, I have witnessed these three distressing phenomena:

1. Staff dismissed without a hearing;
2. Leaders laboring under the misconception that they must never be wrong (or at least never *admit* they are wrong);
3. Fellow workers treating a fallen comrade as a stranger.

When someone is dismissed from a ministry without an appeal, he feels disposable, as a container which, when empty or cracked, is thrown into a dumpster and forgotten. He suspects that his value to the ministry has been only in what he could pour forth or the work he could produce. Being "thrown away" convinces him of his personal insignificance to others.

When this method of dismissal—perfunctorily being told to pack it up and leave—is employed, leadership forfeits an opportunity to do what they should do best—wash the feet of "the least of these . . ." Instead, only a suspicious void exists between them—an unbridgeable gap, a wound of rejection that festers over time.

Denied the hope of ever hearing words of forgiveness and restoration from those with whom he had so recently labored, repentance is all the harder for the one who is under fire. It isn't long before his eyes become filled with the offense of the leadership in not trying to restore him. After all, it is his very life that has been tossed aside! The initial sin becomes lost in the blaming of others.

The sorrow over his losses, the humiliation of dismissal and the leaders' distancing themselves from him obscure the most important issue: his need to repent and be forgiven. God, in His graciousness, will give opportunity for this to happen in other ways later, but great loss of ministry and, more importantly, relationships occurs in the meantime.

Of what is the leadership so afraid that the offender should be sent away in the night? Could it be that sometimes we don't want to risk finding out that perhaps we were wrong in the judgment call? Is human life too troublesome to deal with kindly? Or is it that we fear receiving a smudge on our reputations if redeeming this one should prove messy? How easy it is to be unloving to our own spiritual flesh and blood while being absorbed in loving the lost! It doesn't make sense.

One of my greatest griefs is that the rest of the Body is deprived of beautiful and vital lessons they could learn by watching us do it right. Restoration requires us to relate interpersonally, which involves taking risks to love, being willing to be found wrong in order to reach the truth and sacrificing the safety of our reputation in order to be faithful to a brother. These are issues of maturity that must be taught, and again, taught by example.

Hearings with all involved should be held to determine the accuracy of the charges and the extent of the damage. If the offender has truly repented and appeals for mercy, his appeal should be weighed carefully. Opportunity should be given for him to ask forgiveness of the injured parties and make restitution, if that is possible. Depending upon the nature of the offense, he will likely need to be removed or suspended from his position, allowing for the onset of a plan of constructive discipline.

Counseling is critical for the deep healing of the offender, his family and those offended, especially in the case of sexual sin. This cannot be haphazardly administered; it must be consistent and thorough. Concurrently, mentoring or discipling by a mature believer would teach him how to walk in wisdom in the future.

Forgiveness by his authorities and former coworkers needs to be clearly expressed as early in the process as possible.

Lack of Planning

Every ministry should have a plan in place in the event of sin in the camp, but very few do. When caught by surprise, most ministries just want the offender off the property and out of their lives as soon as possible. Hence, the reputation of many of our ministries: We shoot our wounded.

When a ministry tries to simply forget that a brother ever existed, the rest of us learn only to fear discovery. We carefully erect righteous facades to stave off any penetrating gaze, disassociate ourselves from questionable lambs within the fellowship and avoid being truly vulnerable or truthful to one another, especially to those in authority over us. Revelation of sin is equated with musket fire, so we hide. Our ministries become tinderboxes of mistrust and bitterness.

And so here we are—Catch 22! Everyone is doing to others what he would least desire to be done to himself. We are all caught and contained in the cycle. Seldom is there a divine reunion between the offender and the offended, and after a while, one can't remember which is which!

Pride and fear team up to strip us of faith in God and of the hope of being unconditionally loved by the brethren. We forget that losing our lives (and reputations) in this life, in exchange for finding ourselves at peace with God, is more than a deed done at salvation. It must be continued. Death must be the way of Life.

We would all find ourselves sinning much less if we would be honest and deal with the "little foxes" as they chew away at our branches. Our vision would be clearer. Even a whisper from Jesus would be heard.

We could entertain strangers at a moment's notice, if there were no mounds of dirt under our rugs over which they might stumble. We could wash one another daily with forgiveness and encouragement if we really knew one another and saw our commonality.

We wouldn't need sermons on how to restore a brother if we would each come clean and identify with one another humbly. Restoration would be a natural matter. We would simply do unto others as we would have them do unto us.

What freedom! What generosity! How sensible!

Jesus' younger brother James, who must have known Jesus well, has a word for all our ills: "Confess your sins to each other and pray for each other so that you may be healed" (5:16). I believe that he means that this should be a way of life that not only brings immediate healing but sustains daily health. Paul appeals to us to restore one another gently and to be careful lest we think we are any better. Jesus cautions us not to judge and to love one another just as He has loved us. David beautifully encourages us with a description of the relief found in coming clean and being forgiven of our sins. Even as king, he advocates hiding nothing.

Let's get real about ourselves. Let's forget rank, experience and giftings. None of these things put us above sinning or being responsible to come clean and be made sweet through forgiveness, discipline and restoration.

Finally, Jesus' own prayer would be answered, that we all become one and be known to the world by our love for one another. Can we pray otherwise ourselves and still be in tune with

Him? Can we ostracize, hide, judge and play-act and still be His friends?

If we want to be free, we must own up to our sins and repent, release the bitterness and forgive. We must learn how to bring restoration to our fallen. If we cannot do this without help, we must find that help, for our very lives' sake and the sake of the gospel.

Issues must be faced and examined for counseling, correction and healing to come. As restoration progresses, the past must be forgiven and laid to rest by all of us. This is Body ministry. We are together in this, because what has wounded one, has wounded us all; what teaches one, can teach us all.

We truly are capable of releasing to one another the same love that earmarked the early church. Such love flowing through this aching Body will surely bring us back to full health— even upon *the ledge*!

Personal Note

The call for seasoned, godly leaders to come alongside ministry men and women who are hurt and broken, yet willing to mature, is being answered. In churches here and there across this land, there are leaders who have caught the vision for assisting former colleagues to reach full restoration and a return to their calling within the Body of Christ.

One such leader is Dr. Charles A. Wickman, Senior Pastor of Kempsville Presbyterian Church in Virginia Beach, Virgina. He has designed and implemented in his church a six-month (minimum) pastor-in-residence program for former pastors, missionaries, Christian educators and parachurch personnel.

The program is designed to provide an affirming environment; a mentoring process, which includes comprehensive counseling and accountability; personal ministry opportunities within the church; a re-tooling, educational experience; a place of reference, based on the present rather than the past; and a launching pad from which to be sent back into the ministry when the goals of the program have been reached.

Dr. Wickman's desire is to see this pastor-in-residence program implemented within any evangelical church body that has a vision to reach and restore wounded ministry leaders.

HEARING THE SHEPHERD'S VOICE

See to it that no one misses the grace of God and that no bitter root grows up to cause trouble and defile many. (Hebrews 12:15)

For if you forgive men when they sin against you, your heavenly Father will also forgive you.
        (Matthew 6:14)

You are forgiving and good, O Lord,
   abounding in love to all who call to you.
Teach me your way, O LORD,
   and I will walk in your truth;
give me an undivided heart,
   that I may fear your name.
I will praise you, O Lord my God, with
     all my heart;
   I will glorify your name forever.
For great is your love toward me;

you have delivered me from the
    depths of the grave.
        (Psalm 86:5, 11-13)

I want to know Christ and the power of his resurrection and the fellowship of sharing in his sufferings, becoming like him in his death.
        (Philippians 3:10)

But we have this treasure in jars of clay to show that this all-surpassing power is from God and not from us. We are hard pressed on every side, but not crushed; perplexed, but not in despair; persecuted, but not abandoned; struck down, but not destroyed. We always carry around in our body the death of Jesus, so that the life of Jesus may also be revealed in our body. (2 Corinthians 4:7-10)

I have been crucified with Christ and I no longer live, but Christ lives in me. The life I live in the body, I live by faith in the Son of God, who loved me and gave himself for me. (Galatians 2:20)

Chapter 10

TO KNOW THE CROSS OF JESUS CHRIST

They had heard the story when they were all tiny lambs, still nursing.

There had been a sacrifice—a willing death of one of their own—many years ago. It had been the noblest act of any sheep's life, although it had hurt very much at the time. . . .

"Do you know the Cross of Christ?" the young man intently asked me. I tried to return his probing gaze and answer with confidence, but I couldn't. I had to stall for time. As elementary a question as it seemed, it twisted within me. I probed my heart and spirit for an answer that would satisfy him, and found an ignorance that must be faced.

It slowly dawned upon me that the only crosses I had known were ones of my own mak-

137

ing. If I had suffered for anything, it had been for taking offense when attacked, or because my own independence at times had required a harvest of sorrow. I had deserved every blow. But I had not suffered for being righteous and responding righteously or for unselfishly loving when unloved. I knew little of the cross of Christ, even though I had been saved for 30 years! It was a sobering revelation.

God's answer to my search to know the nature of His cross was to very specifically take three years of my life first to show me how much I needed his forgiveness, and then to reveal to me just how critical it is that I ceaselessly give that forgiveness to others. It was in the giving up control, in considering how I was treated as nothing, losing my life to protect others that I began to know His heart.

In the process, I surrendered my agenda—and the Lord gave to me one that made every single thing that I had ever suffered, all the good and bad that I had ever done useful. He redeemed the past, declaring at an end the hard labor of the flesh as He did for Jerusalem in Isaiah 40:1-2. The price has been paid by Him, and He has taken over my life. He *is* my life. This is the cross!

Power over the Flesh

The cross of Christ alone can bring old patterns of unredeemed behavior to an end. Every time I surrender to His will, which is higher than mine, and die to my own plans, His cross kills the flesh and puts my rebellion into the grave. Then Jesus strangely gives me His life instead. On the other hand, every time I nurse a hurt, judge someone unkindly, seek my own promotion or mock God's authority by not respecting my leaders, I refuse the cross and its power. When my flesh fights for control, my spirit languishes and life becomes miserable.

But when I forgive, when I obey the Lord and trust Him to make sense out of chaos whenever He chooses, peace floods my heart and the burdens are gone. I then find freedom even while in the dungeon!

His grace breaks through and I see the reason for it all: that I know *Him* and experience life through *Him*. Love arrives not a love that grasps, but a love that lets go of self-interest in order to protect and nurture the other one. Faith then miraculously floods my heart, and I am filled with hope!

For me to live is Christ and to die is gain! Not only do I gain heaven someday, but I move out of the restraints of time to touch eternity now. The stress of my expectations is gone. The power of offenses has evaporated into thin air. My sins are gone—forgiven—and any desire for them to return is utterly foreign to my heart. The death of the necessity to sin and its accompanying condemnation has been accomplished. I am no longer my own, but entirely bought by a price which is beyond my comprehension.

All I know is that when I let His cross be mine, when I die to myself and there is no protest left, His peace and power move in. Then *He* lives through me while I fix my eyes securely and only on Him.

He alone—because of the cross and the open grave—could save me from myself. Others can teach me and pray with me, but only He has the power to convict and change me.

At the cross it all began, and at the cross I must stay all the days of my life.

Power to Forgive

The cross brings each of us *forgiveness*. It then calls us to give the same unlimited forgiveness to our fellow men when it makes no "natural" sense at all.

It is during those few brief and far-between moments when we are actually innocent and the other person dead wrong that we even approach knowing the cross of Jesus Christ. Only as we totally release the guilty from any expectation of ours to pay for their crimes do we feel the nails in our own hands. And only as we pour out love upon them in compassion and long to be stepping stones to their seeing the Savior, whatever the cost to our flesh, do we give up the ghost of self and enter His presence.

The Cross . . . is in the heart of the Shepherd as He climbs over rocks and through canyons in the dead of night in search of one rebellious lamb, who, when found, is held fondly and tenderly close and carried to safety.

The Cross . . . is in the life of the pastor who unselfishly serves a tiny, stubborn flock for a lifetime and then dies unnoticed by the world.

The Cross . . . is in the very spirit of the young person who holds no bitterness against parents, teachers or other authority figures, despite the awful mistakes they may have made in handling him as he grows up.

The Cross . . . is in a minister who has no desire to get even with church people who won't forgive him and who slander his name forever.

The Cross . . . is in the obscured, unappreciated and unpromoted staff member who serves tirelessly year after year without jealousy or resentment.

The Cross . . . is in the heart of the pastor's wife who sacrifices security and privacy to follow her husband from charge to charge, never laying claim to a home of her own.

The Cross . . . is in the one who sees beyond faults to the eternal value of his mate and will do nothing to cause that dear one pain or sorrow.

The Cross . . . is in the heart of the one who embraces again the mate who was unfaithful, but has repented and come home. It is in the daily choice to redeem the past together, never blaming, always blessing.

The Cross . . . is in the congregation that allows its pastor to repent openly and, instead of throwing stones, moves in to wisely correct and restore him.

The Cross . . . is in the missionary who serves year after year, with barely a word from home, in order to introduce the Good Shepherd to a people who may yet take his life.

Message for Today

If I were in charge of teaching the next generation how to minister effectively, I would first instruct on the cross. It's His forgiveness at the cross that gives us the courage to face our sins, embrace the Refiner's fire and grow into His likeness. It's our forgiveness of others that generously frees them to learn of Him as well.

We merely *approach* the cross when we cry for a clean heart. We are horrified at the unbroken flesh that is set ablaze when the Refiner's fire replies!

But we *learn* of it as we let Him carry us, absorbing the lessons within adversity, pain and weakness, slowly taking on His strength, forgiving as we have been forgiven.

And then the *joy*—that indescribable joy of knowing Him—swells up and overwhelms us day and night! And we know one thing for certain: To find *Him* has been worth it all!

Without the cross, life on the ledge is insufferable.

With it, our hearts can sing!

THE CROSS

As its shadow gives way
  To hard wood and sharp nails,
My heart screams in fear
  Against the Cross.
To die for my own sins
  Would be a cleansing relief—
  Pour on the pain to this deserving flesh!
But to die for another life—
  Choose to dwell within the pain,
While others around me escape
  With apparent ease,
  Is beyond my comprehension,
  Sucks the very breath from my lungs
  And makes my heart pound with apprehension.
But I cannot run and hide.
A Life beyond myself compels me
  To remain one moment more,
  Bear one sorrow more.
And the pain of the death continues.
  From where will I be sustained forever?
  There is no strength left in this frame!
Lord, You are perfect.
  Your mercy endures forever!
When my soul life surrenders,
  and my selfish heart breaks,
I'll know the Cross at last!

JS

For God's gifts and his call are irrevocable.
(Romans 11:29)

But the plans of the Lord *stand firm forever,*
the purposes of his heart through all
generations. (Psalm 33:11)

I know that you can do all things;
no plan of yours can be thwarted.
(Job 42:2—Job's reply to God)

You did not choose me, but I chose you and ap-
pointed you to go and bear fruit—fruit that will last.
(John 15:16a)

And we know that in all things God works for the
good of those who love him, who have been called
according to his purpose. (Romans 8:28)

To those who have been called, who are loved by God the Father and kept by Jesus Christ:

Mercy, peace and love be yours in abundance.
(Jude 1-2)

Chapter 11

His PLAN

The summer had been dry. The stream dried up in the western region, and no one knew if they would find water in the east.

But the Shepherd never hesitated. Neither drought nor injuries nor predators held him back. They were going on, and none would be left behind. As thirsty as they all were, there was no fear that their hopes would not be realized. They knew that the Shepherd knew, and that was all that mattered.

And they were not disappointed.

God isn't frightened or caught off guard by our failures. His plans for us to mature and radiate His character to the world will move relentlessly on to fulfillment. Even before we were born, we were called to a purpose which He knit into our very hearts, tailor-made to fit.

I have been amazed and humbled by God's persistence in bringing my spiritual dreams to pass. Undaunted by my failures and selfishness, He has set me aright firmly time after time when I have truly repented. In the process, I have learned of the holiness and sovereignty of God.

He is always after our hearts. Until we know that He is God and we are not, and that He alone knows the best way to get things done, we are a danger to any vision He may have for our lives. When there is finally nothing or no one else occupying the place of worship in our hearts, we will be truly used of Him.

He grieves with us over our losses when we move prematurely or in disobedience, and He graciously acts on behalf of those we injure along the way. But then fixes His gaze afresh upon our lives. The correction He brings re-establishes the destined course of His call within our hearts. Like Abram on his journey to becoming Abraham, we learn not to take matters into our own hands in the hopes of helping God fulfill a promise. We learn that He often delays fulfillment of the vision because we need first to know and rest in the fact that His presence is enough to give us joy.

Everything—including the vision—must be surrendered. We must get to the place where we can say that even if it *never* comes to pass, we will be all right, that knowing Him is enough.

The following process is consistently evident in the lives of those who "grow up":

1. God gives us a vision. Passion for it grows in our hearts until it is hard to think of anything else.

2. We become frustrated and restless wondering when God will open the doors and move on our behalf. We begin "helping" Him by promoting ourselves and the vision, pressing hard whenever our authorities or colleagues can't quite seem to get the picture or sense the urgency.

3. We step out on our own, convinced it's the only way to get God's job done. In the process, we judge others and do not seek counsel. We equate the passion in our bones with God's anointing.

4. When the project fails and our zeal is undressed, exposing self-righteousness, we surrender, sometimes in humiliation. The vision essentially dies in our hands, and then we lay it upon the altar. There is sorrow, but God comforts us in the midst of it.

5. As we retreat from others, God begins to reveal the secret, selfish motives that had been in our hearts. We realize that we had taken ownership — and responsibility — for the vision, for which we had absolutely no right nor ability to maintain. Our impatience is revealed as disbelief that God would keep His word to us.

6. Conviction and repentance take us to our knees. We surrender our lives again to Him. Now that He has our attention, He begins to steadily apply pressure in every area of our lives in order to instill integrity and character. Intimacy with

Him becomes our mainstay. Vision for "great things" is forgotten.

7. Others begin to notice a quiet strength in our lives. They are drawn to us for godly counsel, although we hardly notice, for what we *do* is not a priority anymore.

8. The vision appears again as though from the dead! We are cautious this time; we make it a matter of great prayer and ponder it in our hearts, saying little to anyone else. If we are to be involved in its coming to pass, we desperately don't want to soil it with fleshly ambition. God alone will have to bring it about, and it must be confirmed by those who know us best.

9. As we sense God moving on our behalf and preparing us in unique ways, we see clearly that His hand has been in all of it all along. All the stripping and refining were essential preparation for the endurance and maturity level that will be required. We feel very unworthy and inadequate, but we have come to know God and His power. We know that He can bring it to pass and that He can give us a grace and wisdom not our own to fulfill His plans.

10. Ministry comes forth afresh, this time without fleshly ambition, impatience or pride. Humility has been born, out of which will grow fruit that will remain.

God is beneficent, truly, but He is also holy beyond our imagining. Indeed, the common thread binding together all our individual calls is holiness through obedience. His goal for us is that we be "other"—set apart from the systems, voices and loves of this world, to be bound forever only to Him in complete dependence. It is in the release of control of our destinies, dying to dreams as we might fashion them, that His voice begins to matter, that obedience and holiness take root.

It seems that all earthly events for us are meant to cause us to let go, give up, become nothing. As we come to know that His presence is everything— that being without Him is like moving through our days as though in someone else's dream, lonely and pointless—His deepest plans for us unfold. His holiness and His ministry become alive within us! Relationships make sense, the safety of others is paramount, life itself is a privilege and love and trust are treasures to protect. Most amazing of all, we know that we owe it all to Him.

If we have embraced bitterness after our failures and it has settled in with no resistance, perhaps we never knew Him at all! If no brokenness has pursued us, no repentance tugged at us, no sorrow overwhelmed us for those we have hurt, no forgiveness grown within us for those who have treated us unjustly, He is truly a foreigner to us. Perhaps, after all, we never invited Him in. If this is so, cry out to Him for conviction to fall, so that salvation can come!

We who have felt the discipline and breaking within and without are on the right path. We are being drawn on to deeper life in Him and a greater release of His life out from ours. Our dreams are beyond the blueprint stage and under construction.

What He begins, He finishes. This is His character and the essence of faithfulness. We needn't fear being abandoned. We are only learning to hear *and* move by His Spirit. Now when He says to repent, we dash to do it. When He points us to someone who needs our love and compassion, we leave everything to move alongside that person. When He says to forgive, it's an instant act, because the flesh finally files no claim for revenge.

Our dreams and visions have been purified and stripped of self-centeredness, then returned to us as gifts. The destiny fits! We can do nothing but fulfill that destiny!

God has proven again that He is on the throne, and that His faithfulness endures forever. The striving, worrying and running ahead of Him cease. We come to rest.

Then true ministry begins!

The Lord is my shepherd, I shall not
  be in want. . . .
Surely goodness and love will follow me
  all the days of my life,
and I will dwell in the house of the Lord
  forever. (Psalm 23:1, 6)

As the Father has loved me, so have I loved you. Now remain in my love. If you obey my commands, you will remain in my love, just as I have obeyed my Father's commands and remain in his love. I have told you this so that my joy may be in you and that your joy may be complete. My command is this: Love each other as I have loved you. (John 15:9-12)

$\mathcal{B}$eing Prepared

$\mathcal{W}$hen I first joined a ministry staff many years ago, I was welcomed generously and made to feel at home. But it wasn't long before I realized I was on my own. No systematic follow-up was made with me to see that I stayed on track or grew spiritually.

Staff came and went—often in secrecy, disgrace or bitterness. Seldom did someone leave happily. Why did any of these situations have to be? How many problems could have been solved through better communication and early counseling?

These are among the many questions I have asked myself through the years. It has recently occurred to me that I would have been better prepared for the coming experiences if I had asked more questions *initially*. As I recall my employment interviews, I remember answering questions about the skills, education and experience that I was bringing to the job. But I don't remember *asking* many questions.

Questions to Ask

The following are questions we should ask of a ministry before becoming involved:

1. Is the ministry considered more important to the pastor or director than the family? Must I share that philosophy?

2. Does the leader regularly submit himself or herself to another's authority and counsel? Does he or she also seem emotionally healthy?

3. In the case if a parachurch ministry, is it linked to a local church? If so, how much control does the church have over ministry policy?

4. What is the background and character of those persons closest to the leader of the ministry?

5. How often does the staff gather for prayer? What role does prayer have in this ministry?

6. How frequent are staff meetings? May questions be asked during meetings? If not, is there another forum in which questions can be asked?

7. What is the prevailing view of women in this ministry, as established by the director, pastor

or board? What is my immediate supervisor's view?

8. Does leadership conduct periodic performance reviews to encourage strengths and address weaknesses before they become problems? How often?

9. If anyone under my authority or care is abusive to me, will I be protected?

10. What is the route of appeal if I am mistreated by another staff member, particularly my immediate supervisor?

11. What is the process for dismissing a staff member? Would I be given a hearing or opportunity for an appeal before a final decision is made?

12. What will be my specific responsibilities? For a full-time position, can they be performed within a normal workday? For a part-time or volunteer position, can they be performed within a reasonable number of hours?

13. Will I be expected to volunteer extra time on my days or nights off? May I refuse, if necessary, for the sake of my family, without being viewed as lazy, uncommitted or uncooperative?

14. Does the pastor or director practice favoritism?

15. Is professional growth (including promotions) encouraged for women as well as men? Is it based on character and competence,

rather than charisma or connections?

16. Do leaders make it a point to encourage staff?

17. Is the pastor's or director's door always "open" to any staff member who wants to ask a question or offer a suggestion? If so, is it usually respectfully considered?

18. Do I agree with the ministry's doctrinal stance on issues I am likely to encounter?

19. What is the pastor's or director's philosophy of counseling?

20. How does the ministry solicit funds? What is the prevailing attitude and plan when there is a financial shortage?

21. Is the ministry in debt?

Some of these questions could be asked during an interview; others may only be satisfactorily answered through your own observations and the insight of the Holy Spirit. Those in local church leadership or other volunteer positions may need to adapt some of these questions to their situation.

Be Open to God's Leading

Even if all the answers to these questions seem perfect, God may still say, "No, this is not the place for you right now."

Likewise, even if every question brings a dreadful answer, God may say, "Serve here with all your heart. Do it as unto Me alone, keeping your eyes off man, releasing your expectations to Me

daily. Here you will learn many valuable lessons.
Don't worry; I will be with you and sustain you."
In such a case, being aware of the weaknesses in
the fabric of the ministry, ahead of time, can help
you stay emotionally unembattled as God works
in the lives of those around you. Keep your spirit
free from judgment and from being offended;
pray for a move of God to flow—beginning in
you first!

Whatever you do, bathe every move in prayer.
If you think you should change ministries, make
certain that you come to a place of rest first—
content to either go or stay, having put all personal agendas aside. Don't make the move to
escape a difficult situation or to prove anything.
You will take yourself, your judgments and
wounds with you wherever you go. Before long,
the "new" ministry will amazingly smack of all
the flaws of the "old"—because it was *you* who
needed to change, not your ministry!

Never rush! Submit your plans and desires to
your pastor or other spiritual authority and to
your family—then listen to them. Your final
authority is God, but He often uses the people
who know you best to deliver His caution, as well
as His confirmation.

Warning Signs of Weakness

What are the signs that we are poorly prepared
for ministry, that we are immature or even dangerous to ourselves and others as we are? And
what will these weaknesses produce?

- If we haven't learned within family and church life how to surrender our rights and agendas to a more corporate plan, our presence in a ministry will be detrimental. We will be divisive and self-promoting.

- If we haven't offered ourselves to serve others in *any* way they need us, but have rather preferred to tell them what we can do for them, we will find it difficult to lay our lives down for the lost and for our brethren.

- If our devotional life is weak, we will be all the more vulnerable to a quick slide off the ledge of safety. If we have let distance come between us and the Shepherd, we will mistake the hireling's voice for His, be deceived by false teaching and fall into sin.

- If we are slaves to what other people think or expend great energy to constantly please others, we will serve with a divided heart and be easily hurt. We will also be unable to confront sin when necessary, and have a hard time discerning truth.

- If we experience bouts of anger and have not sought counsel to find its roots and gain peace, we will spiritually defile the very people to whom we try to minister, and be in constant friction with God, ourselves and others.

- If we live in constant expectation of others to meet our needs, we will be critical and unfulfilled.

- If our spouses don't want us to be in ministry, if their hearts aren't in agreement with ours, it is likely that we have not learned to meet their needs lovingly and aren't spiritually one with them yet. We must learn to lead and serve unselfishly in our homes first; this is great training for public ministry.

- If we don't understand that God ordained all authority for our protection and that our only job is to obey, we will remain proud and unbroken. We will miss God's loving hand within the fire, as we play His role and judge our authorities. Worse yet, we will teach others to do the same. We will find that our subordinates will ultimately hold us in the same disdain in which they have seen us hold our authorities.

- If we don't really believe God loves us unconditionally, we will become taskmasters over those whom we lead or teach.

- If we think we have to be *perfect* and must never make a mistake, we are self-deceived and will fall into destructive, compulsive behavior. Despair will stalk us.

- If we haven't forgiven fathers who were weak, overbearing or critical, and let God father us instead, we will not know who we are. We will lose hope quickly.

- If we haven't forgiven and blessed our overprotective mothers, we will struggle greatly with trusting ourselves or authority and be forever fearful.

- If we have not forgiven our parents their faults and allowed them to be who they are, good and bad, we will be unable to face our own weaknesses. We will be bound to repeat their failures in our lives and will fall constantly prey to controlling people.

- If we are not in touch with our feelings and repress our emotions, we will become cynical under pressure.

- If women in ministry haven't come to understand the value and dignity of their womanhood and their role as gifted reflections of the character of God, they will be easily intimidated or controlled.

- If men don't grasp the strength in being vulnerable and sensitive to others—as well as firm and confrontational when needed— they will be unable to connect with and deeply minister to others.

- If we don't understand that our authority is given by God, not demanded by us, we will rule as insecure tyrants, constantly fearing rebellion in the ranks, always out of touch with their real needs.

- If we think we deserve credit for the anointing on our ministries, we will be defiled by the applause we crave and fall into tragic sin.

- If we were molested or raped as children or teens and our minds and emotions have not yet experienced deep inner healing, we will be suspicious and unaccepting of real love. We will likely become abusers of others, detached and/or addicted to sexual perversion.

- If ministry brings to our minds thoughts of position and public acclaim, not the faces of hurting people, we do not have the mind of Christ and are not ready for ministry. We need to pray for brokenness and a servant's heart.

- If we like to play favorites within the ministry, we secretly desire their worship.

- If we surround ourselves as leaders with weak, admiring men, we want to be above the law.

- If we are discontent with our spouses and ungrateful for their presence in our lives, we will commit spiritual adultery with someone at work or church.

- If we are committing spiritual adultery and will not repent, we are involved in idolatry and unfaithfulness to God, the ministry and one another. Sexual sin will surely follow.

If any of these patterns are occurring in your life, do whatever is necessary to get free. Every sin, unhealthy attitude or wound will call for repentance and forgiveness at some point. Counseling, discipling or mentoring by a spiritually mature believer can be extremely helpful in building new biblical patterns of thought, belief and behavior.

Don't limp through life; God's deliverance is meant to be thorough and complete! It's time for us to become strong and healthy—especially upon *the ledge.*

Through It All

Here we are, you and I, still in the ministry, still upon *the ledge.* The fire that burns in our hearts to follow the Shepherd has not lessened, but we have gone through so very much on the journey! There has been such intense gratification and joy in seeing lives changed, such wonder at the privilege of being used by God among the brethren, such a deepening of our cry to know Him better and to enter the fellowship of His suffering.

There has also been sorrow, disillusionment, loss, humiliation, betrayal and rejection. We have often stubbornly fed upon the scrubby mesquite bushes at the very rim of the chasm, rebelling against the life He longs for us to live. And we have been frightened and frustrated as we have witnessed others sustain injuries and fall. We have needed forgiveness, and we have experienced the struggle to give that same forgiveness to the rest of the flock.

But, above all, our love for our precious Savior has surged on unabated, and our gratitude for His love is greater than ever! We have entered into a keener, quieter, more disciplined walk of passion than ever before.

We weep more easily and sorrow more deeply over another's weakness; we look more to heaven than to our own "wisdom" for the answers. We don't have as many preconceived ideas or pat solutions for other's problems.

We have learned to hear His voice through one another, and even in the very wind that rushes by! He speaks to us as easily in the stillness of a moonlit night as in an earthquake. And His voice is all that matters.

Our view of God's power and faithfulness in ministering to us and others has vastly increased. We feel as though we have come home. The difficulties are still there, but the struggle is over as we fix our eyes on Jesus, one day at a time.

How did we get to this resting place? What caused us to grow up so much while learning to be as little children? From where has come this strange calm in the midst of the fire, this song from within the center of the blaze?

Why could we never even consider refusing the refining Presence that has become our very life, our very mission, the source of the greatest joy we have ever known? Why do we not mind nor hide the tears anymore? Why do the things of this world mean so little now?

Why? Because *we have been so loved!* We are at a loss to explain this love that does not let us go, this love that nails our flesh to the Cross; this love that rebukes yet defends us, reduces yet fills and satisfies us totally.

We have been so loved, so loved even here—
upon *the ledge.*

ℒamb's Prayer

*Lord, we love You! You surround us and flow
through us, drawing us to life each new day. We
awaken to the sunrise, and You fill us with joy. We
are bathed in blessing with Your presence!*

*You establish our peace and wash away our fears.
With You near, there is no loneliness any night or
day. But our hearts would stop beating and our eyes
close in death, if You took Your mercy from us!*

*You are our life; Your breath in us gives us reason
to live. You shape our heartbeats and pattern our
every move.*

*Your love delights us. You pour it in abundance
upon our thirsty souls, and we long to dance before
You.*

*Our trust is in You forever, for You have loved
us with an everlasting love. Amen.*

Recommended Reading

The Release of the Spirit
by Watchman Nee

A Tale of Three Kings
by Gene Edwards

Why Some Christians Commit Adultery
by John L. Sandford

The Root of the Righteous
by A. W. Tozer